EAT@
HOME

Thank-yous!

Friends and family for their understanding.

All staff at EAT at Dan & Stephs for their help and assistance while we were creating
this cookbook

Pillow Talk Hervey Bay for props.

Krista Graham for her outstanding food styling assistance.

Glen Wilson for photography.

First published in 2014 by New Holland Publishers Pty Ltd
London • Sydney • Auckland

The Chandlery Unit 114 50 Westminster Bridge Road London SE1 7QY United Kingdom
1/66 Gibbes Street Chatswood NSW 2067 Australia
218 Lake Road Northcote Auckland New Zealand

www.newhollandpublishers.com

A record of this book is held at the British Library and the National Library of Australia.

ISBN 9781742575544

Managing director: Fiona Schultz
Publisher: Diane Ward
Project editor: Jodi De Vantier
Designer: Caryanne Cleevely
Photographs: Glen Wilson
Food stylist: Krista Graham
Production director: Olga Dementiev
Printer: Toppan Leefung Printing Ltd

10 9 8 7 6 5 4 3 2 1

Keep up with New Holland Publishers on Facebook
www.facebook.com/NewHollandPublishers

EAT@ HOME

Dan & Steph Mulheron

NEW
HOLLAND

FOREWORD

BY COLIN FASSNIDGE, OWNER OF FOUR FOURTEEN RESTAURANT SYDNEY AND JUDGE FROM MY KITCHEN RULES

Dan and Steph—my friends,

You have embodied everything I look for in good cooks. I love your passion and willingness to learn. I've watched you grow from amateur, passionate cooks who learn on the fly, to now full-blown restaurateurs.

Welcome to my world, and feel the pain!

It's a huge, brave step. I'm very proud of you, and of your first book. You guys are hot on my heels!

I'm honoured to be a part of your journey, and watch the love you have for food and for this industry. You are a couple who have a great love and respect for each other and it's an inspiration to see you doing so well.

Your success is all down to your passion and hard work. I'm delighted to be part of your life and hope I imparted some knowledge along the way.

I hope you enjoy the rest of your food journey as much I have.

LOVE CF (COLIN FASSNIDGE)

CONTENTS

INTRODUCTION

We both love our footy, snags and beer. But make no mistake: we are serious foodies.

After winning the fourth series of *My Kitchen Rules* in 2013, we gained a variety of experiences and many cooking techniques that we use now in our every day life.

We applied to be on the show as we were at a crossroads in our lives. We had been trying IVF to start our family; we worked very hard in our day to day jobs to make ends meet. We rented our house, saved 12 months to go on a holiday every year, so I suppose you could say we were the everyday Aussie battlers.

We weren't great cooks prior to the show, but we would love to entertain our friends and family, we enjoy making people happy with food and we love the preparation of, let's say, a 'service'.

The night of our negative IVF result in 2012, we spoke for hours about what we were going to do next. Then there was an ad on the TV that said 'have you got what it takes to be the next *My Kitchen Rules* champions?' We looked at each other and shrugged our shoulders. Why not? Let's give it a crack. We filled in the online application, then the very next day received a phone call from channel seven. The next five months we endured the lengthy application process, but then we were finally selected. This was the change in our lives we needed. We left our jobs, packed a suitcase each and headed off on this new adventure, neither of us knowing where it was going to take us. It was daunting yet exciting.

The show took six months to film, and each day was between 14 and 16 hours long. We didn't start off that great, but we were sponges; we listened to everything and listened to the judges. We practiced so many different techniques in our small one-bedroom apartment in Sydney. We would baby meat that was in the oven between midnight and 4 am, getting up on the hour every hour to check how it was going. We see now that it was this—the dedication, commitment and hard work—that allowed us to win.

It was an experience of a lifetime and we are so appreciative of every opportunity throughout the show and post-show that has come our way.

It was very overwhelming for us to see how much support we have received and we can't thank everyone enough. Life has changed so much and we are so happy.

We have been together eight years and married five. We both went to the same school. While we knew of each other we didn't associate with each other.

Years went by then and I noticed Steph on Melbourne Cup day at the local pub. I proposed the following Melbourne Cup day and we married the Saturday post-cup day the very next year.

We have a passion for food. 'Dan is the strong cook and always was, prior to the show,' says Steph. 'I wasn't a great cook before we got together. But Dan has taught me so much and is my inspiration.'

'My great love is slow-cooked meat and I make my own sausages. My big passion is snags. I've also got a smokehouse. It's the manly thing to do—smoke stuff. I can't find anything better than a smoked piece of fresh sea mullet,' says Dan.

We unleash our creativity on our friends regularly and get a big rush out of watching people enjoy our food.

We worked extremely hard throughout the competition, stayed a very strong team and had each other's back. They are the main reasons why we are MKR champions. We have big dreams and goals for the future; this is really only the start for us. We are going to make to most of this opportunity. We are not afraid of hard work.

We have recently opened our very own eatery in our home town of Hervey Bay called EAT at Dan and Steph's. The modern menu was created by us and was inspired by our recent trip to the USA.

Our other major goal in the near future is to also start a family. It will happen when it's meant to be Thank you to everyone for their support.

LOVE DAN AND STEPH

BASICS

BASIC WHITE BREAD

MAKES 1

*melted butter, for
    greasing and
    brushing*
*500 g/1 lb plain/all-
    purpose white flour*
2 teaspoons dry yeast
1 teaspoon salt
*375 ml/13 fl oz
    lukewarm water,
    extra water for
    brushing*

HERB BREAD
*¾ cup fresh mixed
    chopped herbs*

FRUIT BREAD
*2 tablespoons
    cinnamon*
1 teaspoon mixed spice
½ cup dried fruit mix
*2 tablespoons brown
    sugar*

There are lots of different types of recipes for bread. Before we went on My Kitchen Rules, we tried to do a crash course on different aspects of cooking. Let me tell you, baking is definitely a science.

Preheat the oven to 200°C/400°F.

Grease a 10 x 20 cm/4 x 7¾ in tin with butter.

Measure the flour, yeast and salt into a large bowl and mix well.

Make a well in the centre and add the lukewarm water. Use a wooden spoon to combine and then use hands to bring the dough together.

Turn the dough onto a lightly floured surface and knead for 8–10 minutes, until smooth and elastic. It will be ready when you press the dough and it springs back a little.

Turn the oven down to the lowest setting so you can sit the dough near the oven to rise.

Shape the dough into a ball, brush a large bowl with melted butter to grease and place the dough in the bowl, rolling the dough around to lightly coat the surface with butter.

Cover with cling wrap then place a wooden board on the oven door with the oven pilot light on. Leave to rise until doubled in size (approximately 45 minutes).

Punch down the dough with your fist. If making the herb or fruit bread, add the extra ingredients for those variations now. Turn the dough onto a floured surface and knead for 3 minutes, until it is elastic and the original size again.

If making bread rolls, divide the dough mixture evenly into your desired size. Roll the balls until smooth and round. Place onto a lined, greased flat baking tray, so they are just touching. Bake in the oven for the same time as the loaf or until they are slightly golden, crispy and sound hollow. Remove and allow to cool. When you are ready to serve, dust with some extra flour.

If you'd prefer to make a loaf of bread, shape the mixture evenly into two balls. Place them side by side into the tin, brush with butter, then place in the warm spot again for 30 minutes until risen, 1 cm/½ in over tin, brush with water and sprinkle poppy seeds.

Bake for 30 minutes. Knock on the bottom of the loaf. If it sounds hollow, your bread is ready. Turn out onto a wire rack while still hot.

BEER BREAD

MAKES 1 LOAF

2 cups plain/all-
purpose flour, sifted
1 cup wholemeal flour
1 tablespoon baking
powder, sifted
1½ teaspoons salt
⅓ cup packed brown
sugar
330 ml/11 fl oz beer of
your choice

Preheat the oven to 180°C/350°F.

Grease a loaf tin with olive oil spray.

In a large bowl, mix together the flours, baking powder, salt and sugar.

Pour in the beer and continue to mix, first using a wooden spoon, then your hands—the batter will be sticky.

Pour into a loaf tin. Bake in the oven for 50 to 60 minutes or until the loaf has browned on top and starts to look crunchy. Knock on the bottom of the loaf—it will sound hollow if it is cooked.

PIZZA DOUGH

MAKES 2 PIZZA BASES

1½ cups plain/all-purpose flour
½ cup self-raising/self-rising flour
1 tablespoon yeast
1 tablespoon salt
¼–½ cup warm water

Sift the flours together in a large bowl then add yeast and salt.

Slowly add the water until the dough comes together.

Place the dough onto a lightly floured surface and knead for 3–4 minutes. Bring back into a ball, it should be soft to touch.

Roll the dough out thinly and place onto an oiled pizza tray, making sure there are no holes and it has a lip on the edge. Top with your choice of pizza toppings. Bake in a 250°C/480°F oven for 15–20 minutes until golden on top.

PASTA DOUGH

MAKES 450 G/1 LB

300 g/10½ oz 'OO'
  flour
3 eggs
pinch of salt

Put the flour and eggs in a food processor and blitz until the mixture comes together and starts to resemble a dough. Add the salt. Bring the dough together in a ball and turn out onto a floured surface.

Knead for 5 minutes or so, until silky, smooth and elastic.

Set up the pasta machine on the widest setting and pass the dough through. Turn and fold the sheet of pasta and pass it through the pasta machine again up to 5 times. Try to keep a rectangular shape to the dough, dusting with flour each time, being sure to coat all the pasta. Start to work the dough through the pasta machine getting to the lowest and thinnest setting, making sure to flour each time

Fold the pasta up into a rectangle, trim the edges and then cut the pasta into small strips or thick strips, whatever you desire, then dust with more flour.

HOMEMADE TOMATO SAUCE

MAKES 1 L/2 PINTS

2 kg/4 lb 6 oz fresh
   tomatoes
bunch of basil
½ bunch of parsley
2 red onions, finely
   diced
2–3 tablespoons red
   wine vinegar
2 tablespoons olive oil
salt and cracked pepper

This will make more than you need for 1 pizza. You can store any leftover sauce in the fridge for up to 7 days or freeze the sauce in an airtight container for up to 1 month.

Place all the ingredients into a large food processor and process until smooth.
   Pour the blended ingredients into a large saucepan, over a medium–high heat. Simmer the sauce for 45 minutes until it becomes thick and a rich red in colour. Taste and season with salt and pepper if necessary. You may need to add a pinch of sugar if the tomatoes are a little acidic.
   Remove from the heat and allow to cool slightly before using as a pizza sauce.

CARAMEL

**MAKES 400-450
ML/14-15 FL OZ**

250 ml/9 fl oz cream
100 ml/3½ fl oz
  glucose
130 g/4½ oz caster/
superfine sugar
25 g/¾ oz unsalted
  butter

This caramel will take your cake or dessert to another level.
I also love to put some salt in this. For the ultimate salted caramel
sauce, add in some good salt flakes and allow to dissolve, then
taste until you reach your preferred saltiness.

Whip cream until soft peaks form.
   Warm glucose in a medium saucepan over a low heat. Once the glucose is
warm, add sugar and stir until dissolved.
   Whisk in the butter and then the cream. Allow to heat and bubble away until
golden and thick.

SEMOLINA BISCUITS

1 cup plain/all-purpose
  flour
¾ teaspoon baking
  powder
¾ teaspoon salt
100 ml/3½ fl oz water
olive oil, to brush
4 teaspoons semolina,
  plus extra for dusting

TOPPINGS
fresh rosemary,
  chopped
szechuan pepper,
  crushed
sea salt
sesame seeds
poppy seeds
cracked black pepper

Sift flour and baking powder into a bowl then add salt. Stir in the water until a firm dough forms.

Knead on a lightly floured surface until smooth. Wrap in cling wrap and set aside for 20 minutes.

Preheat the oven to 180°C/350°F.

Set up a pasta machine and set the widest setting

Feed the dough through until you get to the thinnest setting.

Brush the dough with olive oil and dust with semolina and any other topping that you would like.

Cut into large sheets or use a small rectangular cutter, place onto a baking tray and bake for 7–10 minutes.

Store in an airtight container once cooled.

MAYONNAISE

MAKES 200-250 ML/7-9 FL OZ

3 egg yolks
2 tablespoons white wine vinegar
200 ml/7 fl oz grape seed oil
salt and white pepper, to taste

Whisk egg yolks and white wine vinegar together until mixture becomes pale in colour.

In a slow steady stream, add the grape seed oil while whisking continuously. Whisk until mixture becomes thick and creamy. Check flavour and season with salt and pepper.

Note

You can add different ingredients to this recipe. Stir in some Dijon mustard and tarragon for a French mayonnaise. Add in some roasted garlic for a delicious aioli. Or make a tartare for your seafood dishes using finely chopped pickles, capers, some shallots/scallions and parsley.

BREAKY PIZZA

1 quantity Pizza Dough
    (see recipe p. 17)
Homemade Tomato
    Sauce (see recipe p.
    20)

TOPPINGS
4 oz/120 g sliced ham
4 eggs
Dukkah (see recipe
    below)
good handful of baby
    spinach
parmesan, grated
rocket/arugula
cracked pepper

DUKKAH
almonds, toasted
sesame seeds, toasted
ground coriander
cumin
salt and pepper

To make the dukkah, combine all the ingredients in a food processor and blend until crumbs form.

Preheat the oven to 250°C/480°F.

Roll out the pizza dough, spread the tomato sauce out over the dough. Scrunch up the slices of ham and place them on top of the pizza. This will become cups for the eggs. Add some spinach, sprinkle with parmesan and cracked pepper.

Bake in the oven until the base begins to crisp up and the ham starts to cook. Remove the pizza and crack 4 eggs into the ham pockets. Place back in the oven and bake until the eggs are slightly cooked but still runny.

Slide onto a board and top with rocket scattered over the top. Drizzle with olive oil and sprinkle with dukkah just before serving.

BUTTERMILK WAFFLES
WITH FRUIT COMPOTE, HONEY VANILLA YOGHURT & CINNAMON CRUMB

SERVES 4

BUTTERMILK WAFFLES

3½ cups plain/all-purpose flour
4 teaspoons baking powder
2 teaspoons baking soda
2 teaspoons salt
4 tablespoons caster/superfine sugar
3½ cups buttermilk
1 cup unsalted melted butter
4 eggs
4 teaspooons vanilla extract
olive oil cooking spray

CINNAMON CRUMB

1 cup plain/all-purpose flour
¾ cup brown sugar
¾ cup oats
¾ cup coconut
1–2 tablespoons ground cinnamon
2 teaspoons nutmeg
²/3 cup butter, melted
1 teaspoon vanilla paste

FRUIT COMPOTE

500 g/1 lb apple and pear pieces (about 2 apples and 3 pears)
250 ml/9 fl oz water
100 g/3½ oz caster/superfine sugar
1 teaspoon vanilla bean paste
1 cinnamon stick
zest of 2 lemons

HONEY VANILLA GREEK YOGHURT

250 g/9 oz Greek yoghurt
1–2 tablespoons honey

Combine the dry ingredients in a large bowl.

Whisk the buttermilk, butter, eggs and vanilla together. Pour the wet mixture into the dry mixture and beat well until smooth.

Pour the mixture into a large squeezy bottle or a jug. Grease the waffle iron with oil spray and pour on the batter. Cook for 2 to 3 minutes in total.

To make the fruit compote, combine all the ingredients together in a medium-sized saucepan. Stir the mixture over a medium heat and allow the sugar to dissolve. Bring the mixture to a simmer until the fruit breaks down into the desired consistency.

Make the cinnamon crumb. Stir the melted butter and vanilla together. Combine all dry ingredients together and then pour over the butter mix. Mix everything together and make sure the crumbs are moist.

Put the mixture onto an oiled tray and bake in a preheated oven at 180°C/350°F for 15–20 minutes or until golden.

Mix the yoghurt and honey together.

To serve, place two waffles onto the plate, top with a few tablespoons of compote, a generous sprinkling of crumb and a tablespoon of yoghurt.

EGGS WITH SOLDIERS

SERVES 4

This is the best soft-boiled egg with toast soldiers.

4 eggs
4 pieces of herb bread

Bring a saucepan of water to the boil. Add the eggs and boil for 6 minutes and 15 seconds. Place each egg into an egg cup to serve. Draw a smiling face on the egg shell with non-toxic permanent marker.

Lightly toast each piece of bread and lightly brush them with butter. Slice the bread into strips for the soldiers.

MUSHROOM RAGOUT

SERVES 4

1 kg/2 lb 4 oz button
  mushrooms
500 g/1 lb assorted
  mushrooms
2 tablespoons unsalted
  butter
1 tablespoon coarsely
  milled black pepper
½ tablespoon salt
1 tablespoon dried
  thyme
½ cup cream
bunch of fresh parsley,
  chopped
8 pieces of sourdough,
  toasted
80 g/2½ oz Danish
  feta, crumbled
100 g/3½ oz pine nuts,
  toasted

Place the mushrooms, butter, pepper, salt and dried thyme into a large saucepan and cook the mushrooms, over a medium heat, until softened. Stir in the cream and fresh parsley and heat through.

Lightly toast the sourdough, spread with butter, then spoon on the ragout, crumble over the feta and sprinkle with toasted pine nuts. Serve with a lemon wedge.

STEAK AND EGGS

SERVES 4

BEEF CHEEKS
2 kg/4 lb 6 oz beef
   cheeks
2 x 400 g/14 oz tins
   crushed tomatoes
2 sprigs fresh
   rosemary
1–2 L/4.2 pints
   unsalted beef stock
chopped ends (scraps)
   of carrots, celery,
   onions
4 garlic cloves
salt and cracked pepper

BAKED EGGS
¼ cup beef cheek
   juices, from the beef
   cheeks
200 ml/7 fl oz
   tomatoes, chopped
small handful of baby
   spinach
salt and cracked pepper
8 eggs
parsley, chopped, to
   serve
4 lemon wedges, to
   serve
8 slices of sourdough,
   to serve

Preheat the oven to 150°C/300°F.

Place all ingredients in a large roasting tray and tightly cover with foil. Place in the oven for 4 hours.

Once cooked, allow to sit in the juices, covered, until needed.

Mix the beef cheek juices with the chopped tomatoes. Pour this mixture evenly among 4 small cast-iron pots or medium ramekins.

Add half a beef cheek to each pot. Crack 2 eggs on top of each ramekin and bake in the oven until the eggs are slightly cooked but still runny.

When ready to serve, sprinkle with some freshly chopped parsley and serve with slices of buttered sourdough and a lemon wedge.

CRAB & CORN OMELETTE
WITH CORIANDER HUMMUS

SERVES 4

6 eggs
2 shallots/scallions,
* finely sliced on an*
* angle*
½ cup crab meat
¹/3 cup char-grilled
* corn kernels*
salt and white pepper
lime wedge, to serve

**CORIANDER/
CILANTRO
HUMMUS**
1 x 400 g/14 oz/
* chickpeas, drained*
1 bunch of coriander/
* cilantro*
4 tablespoons olive oil
juice and zest of 1 lime
salt and pepper, to taste

In a bowl, whisk the eggs and a dash of water together until well combined. Heat a large non-stick frying pan over a medium heat. Pour the egg mixture into the pan over a medium heat and cook for 2 minutes.

Sprinkle the shallots, crab meat and corn over the omelette and place under the grill until cooked through.

To make the hummus, place all the ingredients into a food processor and blend until smooth. Add salt and pepper to taste.

Once cooked, slide the omelette onto a plate. Dollop on the hummus and serve with a wedge of lime.

QUINOA BIRCHER

SERVES 4

BIRCHER
1½ cups water
1 cup quinoa
½ cup coconut milk
ground cinnamon, to
* taste*
80 g/2½ oz almonds,
* toasted and roughly*
* chopped*

FRUIT COMPOTE
500 g/1 lb fresh
* seasonal fruit*
* (apple, pear, berries,*
* strawberry and*
* rhubarb), roughly*
* chopped 250 ml/*
* 9 fl oz water*
100 g/3½ oz caster/
* superfine sugar*
1 teaspoon vanilla bean
* paste*
1 cinnamon stick
zest of 2 lemons

Rinse quinoa under running water until the water becomes clear and allow to drain.

Pour water into a medium-sized saucepan and bring to a simmer. Add in the quinoa and simmer for 12 minutes, until the quinoa grains sprout their tails. Turn off heat and leave lid on for 5 minutes to steam, then use a fork to fluff the quinoa and allow to cool.

Place ½ cup of quinoa into 4 bowls and pour over ¼ cup of coconut milk. Sprinkle over the ground cinnamon.

To make the fruit compote, put all the ingredients together in a saucepan. Allow the sugar to dissolve over a medium heat. Simmer the mixture until the fruit breaks down into the desired consistency.

Toast the chopped almonds in a hot oven until lightly browned. Top the coconut quinoa with a heaped tablespoon of compote, then sprinkle with toasted almonds.

ENTRÉES, SIDES & SALADS

QUINOA SALAD

SERVES 4

*250 g/9 oz white
    quinoa, rinsed and
    cooked*
100 g/3½ oz pepitas
*100 g/3½ oz sunflower
    seeds*
80 g/2½ oz sultanas
*80 g/2½ oz rocket/
    arugula or green
    salad mix*
*zest and juice of 1–2
    lemons*
2 tablespoons olive oil
salt and pepper
120 g/4 oz Danish feta

Bring 1½ cups of water to the boil in a large saucepan. Rinse the quinoa under a running tap until the water runs clear and allow to sit and drain.

Add quinoa to the boiling water, cover with the lid until boiling again, reduce heat to a simmer and cook for 12 minutes.

Turn off the heat and leave, covered, for 5 minutes. Remove the lid and fluff with a fork. Allow to cool.

Transfer to a large salad bowl. Add the mixed grains, seeds and sultanas to the quinoa. Add in the rocket or green salad mix.

Make a dressing with the zest and juice of the lemons and oil. Season with salt and pepper. Drizzle the dressing over the salad and toss. Crumble the feta over the top and serve.

TOMATO SALAD

SERVES 4

So easy and so yummy! This is a real treat at a barbecue.

2 truss tomatoes
*4 black heirloom
  tomatoes*
8 slices Serrano ham
4 fresh figs, quartered
*8 large balls of buffalo
  cheese*

Make pesto dressing, by placing all ingredients into a small food processor and blitzing until smooth. Add more oil until the pesto is runny.

Cut up tomatoes and place onto a platter. Roll the ham slices up and put onto the platter. Add the quartered figs. Tear up the buffalo cheese and scatter over the plate. Season with salt and pepper and drizzle with pesto dressing.

BASIL PESTO DRESSING

1 bunch of basil
2–3 garlic cloves
*80–100 g/2½–3½ oz
  pine nuts*
2 tablespoons olive oil
salt and pepper

THAI BEEF SALAD

SERVES 4

250 g/9 oz rump steak
salt
1 tablespoon peanut oil

SALAD
100 g/3½ oz lettuce
  mix
1 carrot, julienned
1 cucumber, sliced into
  ribbons
8 baby grape tomatoes,
  sliced in half
1 long deseeded red
  chilli
¼ bunch of mint
¼ bunch of Thai basil
¼ bunch of coriander
¼ cup chopped toasted
  peanuts

DRESSING
1 tablespoon lime juice
1 tablespoon brown
  sugar
1 tablespoon fish sauce
1 tablespoon sesame oil
1 tablespoon light soy
1 tablespoon finely
  grated ginger
1 garlic clove, chopped

We stumbled upon this great dish in Thailand, but didn't try it (we were a bit funny about the beef). So we waited until we got home to make it and now it's another family favourite.

Add all the dressing ingredients into a small bowl and set aside to infuse and allow the sugar to dissolve. Check the seasoning—there should be a good balance of sweet, sour, salty and spicy.

Rinse the lettuce mixture and drain off the excess water. Put the lettuce, carrot, cucumber, tomatoes and chilli into a large bowl and toss together.

Place your meat in a dry area and let it come to room temperature. Season both sides with salt, place a large pan on to the heat with oil in it and heat until smoking hot. Put in your steak and wait 20 seconds before turning. Cook the meat this way using this method for 3½ minutes and then rest for the same amount of time.

Place your salad mix onto a large plate then place the rested steak onto the salad followed by the fresh herbs and then sprinkle over the toasted peanuts.

BBQ QUAIL WITH PEACH SALAD

SERVES 4

QUAIL
4–8 quails, cut in half length ways
1 teaspoon ground ginger
½ teaspoon cinnamon
large pinch of saffron threads
60 ml/2 fl oz olive oil
2 tablespoons lemon juice

SALAD
8 quail eggs
16 asparagus spears, trimmed
1 tablespoon olive oil
150 g/5 oz bacon rashers, trimmed and cut into 1 cm strips
2 witlof leaves, separated
75 g/2½ oz watercress sprigs
2 peaches, cut into thin wedges
35 g/1¼ oz hazelnuts, toasted and coarsely chopped

DRESSING
1½ tablespoons balsamic vinegar
1 tablespoon maple syrup
60 ml/2 fl oz extra virgin olive oil
salt and pepper, to taste

Cut the quails in half, lengthways.

Combine the ginger, cinnamon, saffron, olive oil and lemon juice in a bowl. Add a pinch of salt and pepper.

Place the quails into the mixture and allow to marinate until ready to barbecue. Keep out of the fridge, so that the meat is at room temperature.

Preheat the barbecue grill to high.

Remove quails from marinade and barbecue, skin side down, for 5–6 minutes or until well browned.

Turn and continue to barbecue for a further 5–6 minutes.

Transfer to a baking tray and loosely cover with foil. Set aside to rest for 5 minutes.

Bring a small saucepan of water to the boil and then reduce heat to low. Carefully add the quail eggs and simmer for 3 minutes.

Remove and cool under cold water. Peel the eggs and cut in half lengthways.

Bring a saucepan of salted water to the boil over medium heat, add the asparagus and cook for 1 minute. Drain and rinse under cold water to stop the cooking process and pat dry with some paper towel.

Bring a saucepan to high heat, add some oil and then add bacon. Fry until crisp, tossing frequently.

Toast the hazelnuts in a hot oven for 5–10 minutes then coarsely chop.

Cut peaches into wedges and separate the witlof leaves.

Make the dressing by combining all ingredients together in a small bowl, stir well to combine. To make the salad, combine all the ingredients in a large flat bowl. Drizzle over the dressing. Place the quail over the top to serve.

VIETNAMESE PORK
WITH VERMICELLI NOODLES

SERVES 4

1 packet vermicelli
noodles
16 cos lettuce leaves
1 cup toasted peanuts,
crushed

MARINATED PORK

1 kg/2 lb 4 oz pork
belly spare ribs
½ bunch of spring
onions/scallions
2 garlic cloves
1 lemongrass stalk
1 tablespoon sesame oil
2 tablespoons fish
sauce
2 tablespoons honey
½ tablespoon white
pepper
1 tablespoon salt

**PICKLED
VEGETABLES**

½–1 cup caster/
superfine sugar (until
right balance)
500 ml/17½ fl oz white
vinegar
1 star anise
¼ green cabbage
1 carrot, julienned

Combine all ingredients, except the pork, in a processor until smooth.

Cover the spare ribs in the marinade and allow to marinate in the fridge overnight. Meanwhile, pickle the vegetables. Dissolve the sugar in the vinegar. You may need to add more sugar to get the balance right. Add in the star anise.

Add the cabbage and carrots and stir to combine. Leave to pickle for 5–10 minutes.

Remove the pork ribs from the fridge and bring to room temperature.

Heat up a barbecue. Cook the ribs on a hot barbecue for 4 minutes on each side—they should caramelise. Allow to rest on a board for 4 minutes, then slice into 1 cm/¼ in pieces.

Cook the vermicelli according to the packet instructions.

To serve, put 4 lettuce leaves on each plate. These will be your 'bowl' for the pork. Add the cooked noodles, sliced pork ribs, pickled vegetables and sprinkle with crushed peanuts.

Serve with sriracha sauce.

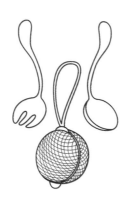

NASI GORENG
WITH CHICKEN DRUMSTICKS

8 drumsticks
2 cm/1 in knob ginger, grated
2 garlic cloves, grated
1 red chilli, finely diced
100 ml/3½ fl oz soy sauce
50–70 ml/1¾–2½ fl oz sweet soy or kecap manis

Anyone that has been to Bali has surely eaten this dish. It's an Indonesian favourite and no wonder, when this delicious dish comes piled high with a runny fried egg on top and a big prawn/shrimp cracker on the side. It's a big hit with tourists too.

Preheat the oven to 180°C/350°F.

Trim the chicken drumsticks and remove the knuckle and skin so you have a clean bone with the meat just at one end.

Mix the ginger, garlic and chilli together in a bowl. In a jug, mix together the soy sauce and sweet soy together until you get the right balance of salty and sweet.

Pour the soy sauce mixture into the ginger, garlic and chilli and stir to combine.

Add the chicken drumsticks to the marinade and leave to marinate for as long as possible. If you don't have much time, give them at least 10–15 minutes and halfway through cooking, baste them again with the marinade.

Place the chicken drumsticks on an oven tray and bake into the oven for 35 minutes, checking regularly, and basting with extra marinade.

Take out of the oven and allow to rest for 5–10 minutes.

Bring a large pot of water to the boil. Wash your rice in a sieve until the water runs clear.

Once the water has boiled, add the rice, cover and bring to the boil again. Reduce heat to a simmer, leaving the lid on the pot. Set a timer for 15 minutes.

After 15 minutes, turn off the heat and allow your rice to steam for 10 minutes but do not take the lid off the pot.

Take lid off and fluff rice with a fork—your rice will be fluffy. Set aside to cool. It's best to have cool or cold rice for nasi goreng, if the rice is hot it will become clumpy and sticky.

Mix the soy sauce and sugar together until you get the right balance of salty and sweet. Set aside.

NASI GORENG

750 ml/24 fl oz water

2 cups white rice

1/3 cup soy sauce

1–2 tablespoons sugar

oil, for frying

2 spring onions/
  scallions, finely sliced

1 onion, finely diced

1 carrot, finely diced

1 teaspoon prawn paste

1 garlic clove, finely
  chopped

1 cm piece ginger,
  grated

5 leaves of Asian
  greens

salt and pepper, to
  season

In a large wok or pot, add oil and heat. Add finely sliced spring onions and fry for 2–3 minutes until crispy. Drain on paper towel for plating.

To the same oil, add onion, carrot and shrimp paste and sauté for 4 minutes to soften. Add the garlic and ginger and sauté for a further 2 minutes. Add the rice and stir through until combined. Then stir through the green leaves. Stir in soy sauce mixture, a little at a time until you get the taste coming through and your rice turns a light brown colour.

Continue to stir-fry your rice and toss in the pan, adding sauce if necessary until all flavours are mixed together well.

Season with salt and pepper to taste.

Using a small bowl, place in some nasi goreng, press down firmly then place your plate on the top and invert—you will have a perfect mound of rice. Place a chicken drumstick next to the mound of nasi goreng and garnish with fried shallots and finely sliced chilli.

You can even top this with a fried runny egg.

55

NASI GORENG WITH CHICKEN DRUMSTICKS

PAELLA

SERVES 4

1–1.5 litres/2 pints salt-
   reduced chicken stock
6 saffron threads
2 tablespoons olive oil
2 chorizo, sliced
1 red capsicum/bell
   pepper, diced into
   chunky pieces
1 brown onion, finely
   diced
3 chicken thigh fillets,
   diced into bite sized
   pieces
3 garlic gloves, finely
   diced
1 tomato, diced
1 tablespoon smoked
   paprika
1–2 teaspoons cayenne
   pepper
2 cups arborio rice
12 green prawns,
   peeled and deveined
salt and pepper, to
   season
1 cup frozen peas,
   defrosted
½–1 cup flat-leaf
   parsley, finely
   chopped
2 lemons, cut into
   wedges, for serving

In a medium-sized saucepan, heat up the chicken stock and add in the saffron threads. Keep warm over a low heat.

Coat a paella pan with olive oil and place over a high heat. Cook the chorizo, capsicum and onion until the onion is soft and the chorizo starts to caramelise.

Add the chicken pieces, garlic, tomato, paprika and cayenne. Cook for a couple of minutes. Stir through the arborio rice and coat well.

Add 2 ladles of warm chicken stock and stir. Let the paella to sit and absorb the liquid. Once you start to see the stock reducing, add a ladleful of stock. Continue this process until the rice is cooked. The paella will become creamy.

Once the rice is almost cooked, add the prawns, pushing them into the rice, allowing them to cook in the heat. Season with salt and pepper to taste. Add peas and a good squeeze of lemon juice. Scatter with chopped parsley and serve with lemon wedges.

BUTTERMILK CHICKEN WINGS
WITH BLUE CHEESE SAUCE

SERVES 4

1 kg/2 lb 4 oz chicken
   wings
3 spring onions/
   scallions, sliced
salt and white pepper
600 ml/21 fl oz
   buttermilk
2 teaspoons smoked
   paprika
1 teaspoon garlic
   powder
½ cup cornflour/
   cornstarch
½ cup plain/all-purpose
   flour

BLUE CHEESE SAUCE

½ cup mayonnaise (see
   recipe, p. 25)
½ cup light sour cream
100–120 g/3½–4 oz
   blue cheese

Place all the chicken wings in an airtight container and roughly stab them with a fork to make small puncture marks. Sprinkle your wings with spring onions, salt, pepper and pour over the buttermilk. Mix with your hands to thoroughly coat. Seal the lid and refrigerate for at least 4 hours (or overnight).

Meanwhile, make the floured coating by mixing the paprika, garlic powder, cornstarch and flour together.

Once your wings have marinated, preheat the oven to 220°C/420°F.

Put the wings in a strainer and leave them to drain for about 5 minutes.

Place the marinated wings into the flour mix and give them a good coating. Dust off any excess flour and place on a lined baking tray.

Bake in the oven for 25 minutes or until golden and cooked through.

To make the blue cheese sauce, combine mayonnaise, sour cream and blue cheese sauce with a pinch of salt and pepper into a small blender and process until smooth. Serve chicken wings with sauce on the side.

MEAT

SESAME CORNED BEEF CROQUETTE,
SOFT BOILED EGG, PICKLED VEGETABLES, WASABI MAYO

SERVES 4

500 g/1 lb corned beef (you
  can purchase shaved
  corned beef from your local
  supermarket), roughly
  chopped
500 g/1 lb potatoes, peeled
  and diced then par boiled
250 ml/9 fl oz White Sauce
  (see recipe, p. 88)
salt and white pepper, to
  taste
½ cup sesame seeds
2 cups panko crumbs
1 cup plain/all-purpose flour
6 eggs, lightly beaten
canola oil, for frying
Mayonnaise (see recipe, p.
  25), for serving
wasabi, for serving

PICKLED VEGETABLES

1 cup white/granulated
  vinegar
½ cup caster/superfine sugar
1 star anise
¼ head of cauliflower, cut
  into florets
1 large carrot, cut into
  julienne strips
5 radishes, cut into small
  wedges

Combine the corned beef, par-boiled potatoes, white sauce and salt and
pepper and mix to combine.

Mix the sesame seeds and panko crumbs together in a bowl. Place the
flour in another bowl and lightly whisk 2 eggs together in a third bowl.

Grab a handful of the corned beef mixture into a rectangular shape. Roll
the patty in the flour. Coat the floured patty in the egg wash and then roll in
the crumb mixture. Repeat with the rest of the corned beef mixture.

Heat up the canola oil in a fryer or a small pot. Use enough oil to cover
the croquette itself. To test if the oil is hot enough, drop a pinch of mixture
into the oil. If it bubbles instantly, the oil is ready. Place the croquettes, one
or two at a time, into the oil and allow to cook until golden brown. Remove
using a slotted spoon and set aside on paper towel. Repeat with the
remaining mixture.

Make some soft-boiled eggs by placing a cold egg into a pot of boiling
water for 6½ minutes and then remove from the water. Run under cold
water until the eggs are cool to the touch and peel off the shell. The center
will be soft and runny.

To make the pickled vegetables, combine the vinegar and sugar until
dissolved. Add the star anise. Leave the mixture to infuse for an hour or
so. Put the vegetables into a large glass jar or airtight container. Pour the
liquid over the vegetables and put into an airtight container to pickle. You
can allow to pickle for up to 3 days and then drain off the liquid. Any pickled
vegetables you don't use straight away will only last another 2 further days.

Mix together the mayonnaise and wasabi to taste.

To serve, place 2 croquettes, a soft-boiled egg, some pickled vegetables
and a dollop of wasabi mayonnaise on each plate.

BEEF CHEEKS WITH
CHORIZO, POLENTA AND BACON CRUMB

SERVES 4

4 beef cheeks
oil, for frying
200 g/7 oz spicy
   chorizo, chopped
1 carrot, diced
1 garlic clove, chopped
1 stick celery, chopped
2 tablespoons tomato
   purée
12 black peppercorns
half a bunch of thyme
1 bottle of red wine
1 litre/2 pints chicken
   stock
1 tablespoons sherry
   vinegar

POLENTA

1.5 litres/1½ pints
   chicken stock
300 g/10½ oz polenta
100 g/3½ oz butter
150 ml/5 fl oz cream
50 g/1¼ oz finely grated
   parmesan

**PARMESAN & BACON
CRUMB**

100 g/3½ oz bacon, finely
   diced
½ cup panko breadcrumbs
100 g/3½ oz parmesan
   cheese, grated
salt and pepper
1–2 tablespoons fresh
   parsley, finely chopped

Cut the beef cheeks in half and trim.

Heat some oil in a casserole pot over a medium–high heat and seal the meat on all sides. Remove and set aside.

Add the chorizo to the same pot and fry until crispy, then remove.

Add the carrot, garlic and celery and cook on a low heat for 5 minutes. Stir in the tomato purée, peppercorns and thyme. Pour in the wine and stir well. Bring to the boil and cook for 15 minutes.

Add the beef cheeks and chorizo back into the pot and pour in stock. Return to a simmer then cover with lid

Simmer, covered, for 2½ hours.

Stir in the sherry vinegar just before serving.

To make the polenta, bring the stock to the boil in a large saucepan. Gradually add the polenta, stirring well. Cook for 5 minutes.

Stir in the butter, cream and parmesan cheese, then cook for another 5 minutes.

To make the parmesan and bacon crumb, fry the bacon over a medium–high heat until golden brown. Stir in the breadcrumbs and remove from the heat. Stir in the parmesan cheese, salt, pepper and parsley.

Serve a beef cheek with a side of polenta. Sprinkle over the parmesan and bacon crumb.

CABERNET BRAISED BEEF WITH
HERBED PARMESAN POLENTA CAKE & BRUSSELS SPROUTS

SERVES 4

BRAISED BEEF

2 tablespoons plain/all-
  purpose flour
salt and pepper
2 kg/4 lb 6 oz chuck
  steak or stewing
  steak, cubed
2 tablespoons olive oil
1 brown onion, diced
2 garlic cloves, crushed
2 carrots, peeled and
  sliced
6 mushrooms, sliced
2/3 cup red wine
1 litre/2 pints salt-
  reduced beef stock
2 large brushed
  potatoes, peeled and
  diced
6–8 Brussels sprouts
fresh parsley, chopped

Season the flour with a pinch of salt and pepper. Toss beef pieces through and coat.

Add olive oil to a large pot over a high heat. Cook the beef pieces until golden—remove from the pan.

Add the onion, garlic, mushrooms and carrots. Sauté for 2 minutes.

Pour in 2/3 cup of red wine to deglaze the pan, stirring to scrap the bottom of the pan for the flavours.

Reduce the heat to low, pour in the stock and bring to a slow simmer.

Add beef pieces and cook, covered, slow and low, for 2 hours, stirring occasionally.

Make sure that there is always enough liquid in the pot to cover the meat, top with water if becoming low. After 1 hour and 40 minutes, add the potato and cook until tender in the juices.

Season the dish with salt and cracked pepper to taste.

To make the polenta cake, line the base and sides of a large rectangular or square pan.

Bring the stock to the boil in a large pot and reduce the heat to low. Add the polenta slowly, whisking constantly, until well combined.

Cook, stirring with a spoon for up to 5 minutes or until thickened. Stir in fresh herbs, parmesan, butter and salt and pepper to taste.

Pour into the lined tray, smooth the surface and allow to cool.

Cover and place in the fridge for up to 2 hours to set.

Just before you are ready to serve, heat up a grill pan.

Cut the cooled polenta into rectangular pieces.

Brush both sides with olive oil and cook on the hot grill until charred. Turn over to grill the other side.

POLENTA CAKE

170 g/6 oz instant polenta
1 litre/2 pints salt-reduced vegetable stock
2 tablespoons freshly chopped rosemary
2 tablespoons freshly chopped oregano
1/3 cup parmesan cheese
salt and white pepper
1 tablespoon unsalted butter
olive oil

Trim each Brussels sprout. Bring a pot of salted water to the boil and blanch the sprouts for 3–4 minutes. Remove and refresh in a bowl of cold water to stop the cooking process.

Once cooled slightly, peel each leaf of the sprouts, they will be placed over the dish at serving.

To serve, place some grilled polenta cakes onto each plate, top with some braised beef, some sprout leaves and sprinkle with fresh chopped parsley and a drizzle of olive oil.

BALSAMIC ROASTED MUSHROOM
RISOTTO WITH PEPPERED RIB FILLET

SERVES 4

RIB FILLET
*4 x 200 g/7 oz rib
   fillets, 2 cm/1 in thick*
salt
olive oil
cracked pepper

RISOTTO
*200 g/7 oz button
   mushrooms, sliced*
*3 garlic cloves, thinly
   sliced*
*2 teaspoons fresh
   rosemary, chopped*
2 tablespoons olive oil
*1 tablespoon balsamic
   vinegar*
3–4 cups chicken stock
*2 spring onions/
   scallions*
1 cup arborio rice
¼ cup dry white wine
1 tablespoon butter
*80–100 g/2½–3½
   oz freshly grated
   parmesan cheese*
*salt and pepper, to
   season*

Preheat the oven to 180°C/350°F. Line a roasting tray with baking paper.

Combine the sliced mushrooms with the garlic and rosemary. Toss with a drizzle of olive oil and balsamic vinegar. Place onto a lined roasting tray and roast for 20 minutes.

Add stock to a saucepan on a medium low and warm through.

Heat remaining oil in a pan on medium heat. Sauté spring onions for 1 minute. Add rice and stir until all coated. Cook for about 2 minutes.

Pour in wine and stir until fully absorbed.

Add stock to rice, ½ cup at a time, stirring continuously until absorbed. Continue this process until the rice is al dente.

Stir in the mushrooms and juices from the roasting pan. Remove from heat, stir in the butter and cheese. Season to taste.

Place a grill pan on a high heat and wait until it is smoking.

Rub steak with some olive oil and season with a couple of pinches of salt.

Once the pan is smoking, spray on a small amount of oil and then place the steak on the grill. Leave for 20 seconds and then turn. Continue to turn the steak every 20 seconds for 4 minutes in total.

Take off the grill and allow to rest for 3–4 minutes—resting is important as it allows the meat to relax and seal in all juices before slicing.

While resting, crack black pepper over each side. Cook the remaining fillets the same way.

Mould a tall amount of risotto in the middle of the plate. Slice the steak and place pieces of steak to one side of the risotto.

Garnish with fresh rosemary and more parmesan.

BACON AND MUSHROOM
STUFFED ROLLED BRISKET

SERVES 4

1 tablespoon olive oil

½ brown onion, diced

200 g/7 oz bacon, diced

200 g/7 oz mushrooms, chopped

1 garlic clove, crushed

1 tablespoon unsalted butter

2 tablespoons parmesan, grated

2 tablespoons panko breadcrumbs

2 tablespoons chives, chopped

salt and cracked black pepper

1 kg/2 lb 3 oz flat brisket

asparagus spears

juice of ½ lemon

drizzle of olive oil

salt and white pepper

CORN PUREE

4 corn cobs

3–4 tablespoons cream cheese

½ teaspoon smoked paprika

salt and pepper to taste

Preheat the oven to 150°C/300°F.

In a frying pan, heat some olive oil over a heat high. Cook the onion, bacon and mushrooms. Sauté until the bacon starts to crisp up and the onions and mushrooms soften. Add garlic and butter. Continue to cook until softened. Remove from the heat and stir through the parmesan, panko crumbs, chives and season to taste.

Spread mixture evenly over the non-skin side of the brisket, then roll up the meat. Tie the brisket together with string, at 2 cm/1 in intervals.

In the same frying pan you just used, heat some olive oil over a medium heat and brown all sides of the brisket.

Place the browned brisket on an oiled baking tray and roast in the oven for 1 hour and 30 minutes.

Remove from oven, turn brisket over and place back into oven and cook for 1 hour. Once cooked, remove from oven and allow to rest for 20 minutes.

Meanwhile, make the corn puree by char-grilling 2 corn cobs under the grill until slightly browned. Remove from the grill and allow to cool slightly. Blanch the remaining corn cobs in a pot of water until tender, allow to cool.

Once the corn cobs have cooled, cut off the kernels.

Place corn, creamed cheese and paprika into a processor and blend until smooth. Season to taste.

Make a gravy for the meat by straining all juices from the brisket pan, using a fine sieve, catching the liquid in a small saucepan. With this juice, add ½–1 cup of water, place on medium to high heat and reduce to a thick sauce.

Bring a pot of water to the boil. Cook the asparagus in the boiling water for 2–3 minutes or until just crisp, then remove with a slotted spoon.

Dress the cooked asparagus with some olive oil, fresh lemon juice and salt and white pepper.

Just before serving, put the puree into a small saucepan over a low heat and stir through until smooth.

To serve, slice the brisket into 1.5 cm/½ in pieces. Smear some corn puree over each plate.

Place brisket on top of the puree, then top with asparagus and spoon over some reduced sauce.

BRAISED BEEF SHORT RIBS
IN UNDER AN HOUR!

SERVES 4-6

1 bunch baby bok choy,
 sliced lengthways into
 quarters
1 red capsicum/bell
 pepper, sliced
200 g/7 oz snow peas
1 tablespoon peanut oil
1 small hot chilli, finely
 sliced
2 spring onions/
 scallions, finely
 chopped, for serving
sesame seeds, toasted,
 for serving

BEEF SHORT RIBS

1 kg/2 lb 4 oz beef short
 ribs
2–4 tablespoons plain/
 all-purpose flour
1 tablespoon sesame oil
2 brown onions,
 coarsely chopped
4 red hot chillies,
 chopped
3 tablespoons hoisin
 sauce
2 tablespoons soy sauce
250 ml/9 fl oz beef
 stock
1 tablespoon balsamic
 vinegar
250 g/9 oz pitted prunes
salt and pepper

Coat the ribs in the flour.

Put the sesame oil, onions, ribs and chillies into a pressure cooker. Stir to combine, making sure the ribs are coated.

Add hoisin, soy, stock, balsamic and prunes. Stir to combine.

Lock the lid of the pressure cooker and bring to high pressure over high heat. Cook for 35 minutes, adjusting the heat if necessary.

Once done, remove from the heat and let the pressure out of the cooker.

Slowly release the lid, check to see if the ribs are tender. If not, lock the lid again and return to pressure again for another 5 minutes. Transfer the ribs to a bowl.

Bring the sauce in the pot to a boil and boil until the sauce thickens. Season to taste, then strain.

Place ribs and prunes back into pot and cover with sauce.

Bring a large wok or saucepan of water to the boil.

Add the bok choy and capsicum into a bamboo steamer and place over the boiling water. Steam for 3–4 minutes, then add the snow peas and then continue to steam everything for a further 2–3 minutes.

Once cooked, transfer to a warm frying pan. Add peanut oil, then add some sauce from the ribs mixture to the vegetables and toss through to stir-fry.

To serve, place the stir-fried vegetables onto a plate. Place ribs with some extra sauce onto the greens. Garnish with sliced chilli, spring onions and sesame seeds.

GRILLED BEEF CAP
WITH CELERIAC & HORSERADISH REMOULADE

SERVES 4

1.5 kg/3 lb top sirloin
  rump cap (or
  picanha)
500 g/1 lb salt
5 tablespoons black
  cracked pepper
1 tablespoon garlic
  powder
1 teaspoon dried thyme
1 teaspoon dried
  oregano

REMOULADE
100 ml/3½ fl oz
  whipping cream
125 ml/4 fl oz
  mayonnaise
4 tablespoons
  horseradish, freshly
  grated
1 celeriac, trimmed
  & sliced into thin
  battons
1 Granny Smith apple,
  peeled & sliced into
  thin battons
½ red onion, finely
  diced
salt & pepper
juice of ½ lemon
small bunch of
  watercress sprigs

Take the meat out of the fridge and bring to room temperature before cooking. Preheat the oven to 250°C/480°F.

Mix all dried herbs, garlic powder and salt together.

Line the base and sides of a baking pan with double foil. Pour half the salt mixture on the bottom of the tray. Add the rump on top with the fatty side facing down. Cover the meat with the other half of the salt.

Place into the oven and roast, uncovered, until the center of the meat reads 50°C/122°F (this will be rare). It may take 30 minutes for the meat to be rare.

Take the meat out of the oven, lift the meat out of pan and place onto a rack. Leave to rest for 10 minutes and then carve into 1 cm-thick slices.

To make the roulade, whip the cream until soft peaks form and then gently fold through the mayonnaise.

Add freshly grated horseradish and fold through, making sure there is a real good hit of horseradish in there. Finish with some salt and pepper.

Fold this cream through the celeriac, apple, red onion and lemon juice. Taste and season if needed. Carefully fold through the watercress.

To serve, place some meat on each plate and add a mound of remoulade and a cheek of lemon. Serve immediately.

ROAST CHICKEN
WITH LEMON AND THYME STUFFING

SERVES 4

CHICKEN STOCK
3 kg/6 lb 10 oz chicken
 carcass pieces
60 ml/2 fl oz vegetable
 oil
2 brown onions,
 coarsely chopped
1 leek, white part only,
 coarsely chopped
2 celery stalks,
 coarsely chopped
2 carrots, unpeeled and
 coarsely chopped
½ bunch thyme
4 bay leaves
½ teaspoon black
 peppercorns
5 litres/10½ pints
 water

1.5 kg/3 lb 5 oz whole
 chicken
60 ml/2 fl oz extra
 virgin olive oil
1 large brown onion,
 finely chopped
2 garlic cloves, crushed
160 g/5½ oz fresh
 breadcrumbs, made
 from crusty bread
2 tablespoons flat-leaf
 parsley, chopped

Firstly, start with the chicken stock. Preheat the oven to 200°C/400°F.

Wash the chicken pieces and place into a large roasting pan. Drizzle with oil. Roast for 20 minutes then turn bones over and roast for a further 20 minutes until a dark golden brown. Remove from the oven and set aside.

Heat the oil in a large stockpot over a medium heat and cook all the vegetables for about 10 minutes, stirring frequently to ensure they are evenly browned.

Add the chicken pieces, herbs, peppercorns and enough water to cover all ingredients.

Bring to the boil over a high heat. Reduce the heat and simmer gently for as long as possible, but a minimum of 2 hours. Skim the surface regularly to remove any fats. Remove from heat and leave to cool slightly.

Ladle through a fine sieve into a clean container and set aside until needed for the gravy. Before adding to the gravy, be sure to remove any fats that may have solidified on the surface.

Preheat the oven to 200°C/400°F.

Wash the whole chicken under cold running water. Trim off the neck, giblets and any fat, then pat dry with paper towel and set aside.

Heat oil in a large frying pan over medium heat and cook the onion, stirring often, for 5–6 minutes or until softened. Add the garlic and cook for 1 minute. Transfer to a bowl.

Add the breadcrumbs, parsley, lemon zest, thyme, salt and pepper and mix until well combined.

Spoon the stuffing into the chicken cavity, stuffing it until firm. Pull the skin on either side of the cavity together, then secure by threading a small thin metal skewer through several times.

Rub the chicken with some olive oil then season with salt and freshly ground pepper.

zest of 1 lemon

3 teaspoons thyme

variety of vegetables,
   steamed (snow peas,
   sugar snap peas and
   asparagus are a good
   choice)

ROAST POTATOES

4 large désirée
   potatoes, peeled and
   quartered

salt

water

olive oil

GRAVY

1½ tablespoons plain/
   all-purpose flour

500 ml/17½ fl oz
   chicken stock (see
   recipe p. 84)

juices from the roast
   chicken

Truss the legs with kitchen string

Put the chicken into a small roasting pan and roast for 15 minutes.

Reduce the heat to 180°C/350°F and roast for another 45 minutes or until the juices run clear when you pierce the chicken through the thickest part.

Transfer to a warm plate and cover loosely with foil and leave to rest.

Bring a large saucepan of salted water to the boil, add the potatoes and cook for 5–6 minutes. Drain and cool slightly.

Using a fork, gently rake the surface of each potato. Place the potatoes in a roasting pan in a single layer, then drizzle a generous amount of olive oil over to coat.

Roast in the same 200°C/400°F oven as the chicken for 50 minutes or until deep golden and crisp. Season with salt and pepper once out of the oven.

Make the gravy in the same pan that the chicken was in. Place the pan on the stove top over a medium heat.

Add the flour and cook, stirring, with a wooden spoon for 3–4 minutes, until smooth.

Gradually add the stock and whisk constantly. Reduce to a simmer between additions of stock to prevent lumps.

Once all the stock has been added, simmer for 2–3 minutes until thickened and smooth.

Season with salt and pepper and then strain into a warmed jug ready to serve.

Trim the vegetables to the same size. Steam for a few minutes together, until crisp.

Serve the roast chicken, potatoes and steamed vegetables covered with the gravy.

CORNED BEEF, CONFIT POTATO
AND HONEY CARROT PUREE

SERVES 4

CORNED BEEF

1.5–2 kg/3 lb 5 oz–4 lb 6 oz corned beef/silverside
water, enough to cover the meat when it is in the pot
¼ cup brown vinegar
1 bay leaf
1 tablespoon whole peppercorns

CONFIT POTATOES

12 kipfler potatoes, peeled and cut into 2 cm/1 in thick pieces/discs
300 g/10½ oz duck fat or 500 ml/17½ fl oz olive oil
4 sprigs of thyme
2 garlic cloves
pinch of salt

This has got to be a family favourite all around Australia. Put it on in the morning and the smell will waft through the whole house.

Dan: This smell reminds me of when I was young, and we'd come home from footy on a Sunday.

Steph: Every time we went to visit my nana at her home, there was always a plate of corned beef in the fridge for us kids to eat. It wasn't that flash, but we loved it. We always had it served with boiled potatoes, boiled cabbage and white sauce with parsley. This dish is so comforting to me.

Place the corned beef in a large pot together with water, vinegar, bay leaf, and peppercorns. Cover with a lid and bring to the boil. Reduce heat to a low simmer to cook for 1–1½ hours.

Remove from water and allow to rest for 10 minutes and then slice into thin slices, against the grain.

Make the confit potatoes by placing the sliced potatoes, duck fat, thyme, garlic and salt into a heatproof, vacuum-sealed bag, expel the air and seal.

Bring a large pot of water to the boil and then reduce to a simmer. Place the bag of potatoes into the simmering water and cook for 45 minutes.

Open the bag and drain the potatoes from the fat.

Recipe cont.

CORNED BEEF, CONFIT POTATO
CONT.

HONEY CARROT PUREE

6 large carrots, peeled and sliced
4 tablespoons butter
3–4 tablespoons honey
salt and pepper, to taste

WHITE SAUCE

2 tablespoons butter
2 tablespoons plain/all-purpose flour
1 cup milk, warmed
salt and white pepper, to taste
¼ cup fresh parsley, chopped

Over a medium heat, in a medium-sized saucepan, cook the carrots in a little water, with butter and salt until the carrots are soft and the water has evaporated. Increase the heat and add the honey. Caramelise the carrots slightly. Remove from the heat and place carrots into a blender or food processor and puree until a smooth consistency. Add salt and pepper to taste

To make the white sauce, melt the butter in a saucepan over medium heat. add flour and stir until mixture is well combined.

Gradually stir in the warm milk and cook over medium heat, stirring constantly until the sauce begins to thicken. Season to taste. Add fresh parsley and stir.

To serve, place some corned beef on each plate with a side of potato, some carrot puree and pour over the white sauce.

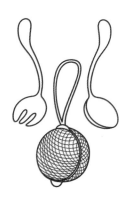

CRUSTED PORK CUTLET WITH
APPLE SLAW AND SALSA VERDE

SERVES 4

4 pork cutlets
4 lemon cheeks, to
  serve

CRUST

4 thick slices of
  sourdough bread
large handful of parsley
2 garlic cloves
2 sprigs of thyme
½ cup parmesan,
  freshly grated
zest of 1 lemon
salt and pepper
3 eggs
2 cups plain/all-
  purpose flour
4 tablespoons extra
  virgin olive oil

MAYONNAISE

3 egg yolks
2 teaspoons white wine
  vinegar
2 tablespoons whole
  seeded mustard
200 ml/7 fl oz grape
  seed oil
salt, to season
white pepper, to season

This recipe we will alway remember creating in our little apartment when we were about halfway through MKR. We had learned a lot through the show and we went to visit a well-respected butcher shop in Sydney called Victor Churchill. While we were there we got chatting to the amazing staff about meat and about cleaning the bones (handles!) of the meat prior to cooking.

The flavours of this dish are fresh and vibrant—we absolutely love it.

Preheat the oven to 180°C/350°F.

Take the pork cutlets out of the fridge so they start to get to room temperature. Clean up the bones so they are free of meat and look clean.

Put the sourdough bread, parsley, garlic, thyme, parmesan, lemon zest and salt and pepper into a food processor and pulse together until you have fine bread crumbs. Spread onto a plate and set aside.

Lightly beat the eggs in a bowl and set aside.

Season the flour on a plate with salt and pepper and set aside.

Take your cutlets and lightly flour the bottom half of the cutlet, then dip this bottom half into the beaten egg, followed by the breadcrumbs—only half the cutlet will be crumbed.

In a hot fry pan, add extra virgin olive oil. Fry the cutlets for 2 minutes on each side, until the crust is golden brown, then place onto an oiled baking rack and bake in the oven for 5 minutes. Remove and allow to rest for 5 minutes.

Recipe cont.

CRUSTED PORK CUTLET
CONT.

APPLE SLAW

½ celeriac, peeled and
   julienned
2 pink lady apples
60 ml/2 fl oz lemon
   juice, freshly
   squeezed
1 tablespoon fresh
   mayonnaise
2 tablespoons
   wholegrain mustard
1 spring onion/
   scallions, finely
   chopped
2 tablespoons chives,
   chopped
zest of ½ a lemon

SALSA VERDE

1 large bunch tarragon
2 tablespoons parsley,
   chopped
1 tablespoon capers
1 tablespoon balsamic
   vinegar
juice of 1 lemon
1–2 tablespoon olive oil

Place egg yolks, vinegar and mustard in a bowl and, using an electric whisk, blend until all the ingredients are light and creamy.

While whisk is still running, gradually add the grapeseed oil in a slow steady stream until the mayonnaise is thick and pale. Season with salt and pepper to taste. Lastly, stir through whole seeded mustard.

Peel and finely julienne the celeriac. Core and quarter the apples and finely slice with a mandolin. Gently toss together in a large bowl with celeriac and fresh lemon juice.

Add the mayonnaise, the mustard, spring onions, chives and lemon zest and stir to combine. Season with salt and pepper and set aside.

Place all the salsa verde ingredients into a small food processor. Add enough oil to make a spoonable, but thick, salsa verde.

To serve, place the pork onto a plate with a nice mound of apple slaw next to the meat and then a few good dollops of salsa verde next to the meat for dipping.

SLOW-COOKED LAMB SHOULDER
WITH CHORIZO AND WHITE BEANS

SERVES 4

2 tablespoons
  rosemary, chopped
2 tablespoons oregano,
  chopped
1 tablespoon thyme,
  chopped
2 garlic cloves, chopped
1 teaspoon fennel seeds
60 ml/2 fl oz olive oil
salt and pepper, to taste
1 kg/2 lb 3 oz boned
  shoulder of lamb
2 chorizo sausages, cut
  into 1 cm/¼ in thick
  slices
125 ml/4 fl oz dry
  white wine
125 ml/4 fl oz chicken
  stock
2 x 400 g/14 fl oz
  cans cannellini beans,
  drained and rinsed
2 tablespoons butter
salt and pepper

PARSLEY PUREE
1 cup firmly packed flat-
  leaf parsley
2 garlic cloves
2 tablespoons lemon
  juice
1 teaspoon Dijon
  mustard
60 ml/2 fl oz olive oil

Put all the parsley puree ingredients into a food processor and process until smooth. Season with salt and pepper to taste. Cover and set aside.

Preheat the oven to 130°C/260°F.

Place the rosemary, oregano, thyme, garlic and fennel seeds into a small processor and process until finely chopped.

Add 2 tablespoons of oil, season with salt and pepper and process until a paste forms.

Place the deboned lamb on a large plate and brush all over with this paste.

Heat the remaining oil in a heavy based flameproof casserole dish over medium heat and cook the chorizo for 3 minutes, until browned on both sides then remove and drain any excess oil from dish.

Place the lamb in the casserole dish and pour in the wine and stock.

Bring to a boil over high heat then return the chorizo to the dish, cover, and cook in the oven for 4 hours.

Remove the lamb from the dish and allow to rest for 30 minutes. Carve into serving portions.

Drain the cannellini beans and heat in a pan with some butter, once warm through roughly mash the beans and season.

Place the lamb into shallow serving bowls and spoon over some sauce from the cooking pan. Place a good spoonful of smashed cannellini beans and top with parsley puree.

LAMB KOFTAS & ZESTY COUSCOUS
WITH HONEY MINT YOGHURT

SERVES 4

baby cos lettuce hearts
250 g/9 oz yoghurt
1–2 tablespoons honey
small bunch of mint,
*   chopped*
pinch of salt

KOFTAS

500 g/1 lb lamb mince
2 tablespoons thyme
1 tablespoon ground
*   chilli*
1 tablespoon ground
*   cumin*
1 tablespoon sumac
zest of 1 lemon
½–1 red onion, finely
*   diced*
1 teaspoon each salt
*   and pepper*

COUSCOUS

2 cups chicken or
*   vegetable stock*
1½ cups cous cous
100 g/3½ oz Danish
*   feta*
small bunch mint
*   leaves, chopped*
80 g/2½ oz pine nuts,
*   toasted*
1 pomegranate, seeds
*   only or 1 cucumber,*
*   seeded and diced*

80 g/2½ oz baby rocket
small bunch of chives,
*   chopped*
juice of 1 lemon and zest
olive oil
salt and pepper

To make the koftas, combine the ingredients together and set aside to allow the flavours to infuse for a while.

Mould a small handful of the mince between your fist to make the kofta. Repeat with the remaining mixture. Cook on a hot grill until charred and cooked through.

To make the couscous, bring stock to a boil in a medium-sized saucepan then turn off heat. Add the couscous, stir quickly and cover with a lid until the couscous has absorbed all the liquid. Fluff with a fork and allow to cool.

Place the couscous in a bowl, add in the rest of the ingredients and toss together. Season with olive oil, lemon juice and salt and pepper.

In a small bowl, mix together the yoghurt, honey and mint. Season to taste.

We like to eat this dish by putting a scoop of the couscous, a kofta ball and some yoghurt in a lettuce cup and enjoying it like a Middle Eastern taco. But you could also serve this on a plate with a few koftas over a bed of couscous, with the honey mint yoghurt on the side.

BACON TERRINE

SERVES 4

1 thick slice of white
    bread
1 small onion, roughly
    chopped
2 cloves garlic,
    squashed
4 fresh sage leaves
1 sprig fresh thyme,
    leaves removed
225 g/8 oz pork mince
225 g/8 oz pigs liver,
    trimmed
75 g/2½ oz thick
    chunks of bacon
    (2 x 2 cm/1 x 1 in)
4 tablespoons apple
    juice
9–12 streaky bacon
    rashers
extra sage leaves and
    thyme sprigs, to line
    tin

This is a great terrine that can be served in heaps of different ways. Dish it up at breakfast with a runny egg and some toast or try it at lunch on a burger—this is delicious with dill pickle or chutney.

Preheat the oven to 160ºC/320°F.

Place the slice of bread, onion, garlic and herbs into a food processor and blend together until the mixture is fine crumbs.

Add the pork mince and liver and process until the mixture is smooth. Transfer to a bowl. Stir in the thick chunks of bacon and the apple juice.

Using a 1 L/2 pt terrine/loaf tin, line the bottom of the tin with 4–5 streaky bacon rashers line the bottom of the tin, making sure you have enough on each side to fold over the top.

Place some sage leaves and thyme onto the rashers.

Fill with half the raw meat mixture and line with 3–4 bacon rashers lengthways. This time then add more herbs to cover the mixture.

Add some more rashers, length ways again and then fold over the other rashers, so it's a tight little parcel

Place the filled terrine into a roasting pan and half-fill the roasting tin with boiling water. Cover with a piece of greased foil and place in a preheated oven. Cook for 1½ hours until the mixture is set and cooked through.

Allow to cool.

SAUSAGES

Making sausages at home is not as daunting as you may think. In fact, it is very rewarding. The best thing about making homemade sausages is that you know exactly what goes into them. Once you get the hang of the basics, you can experiment with many different flavours.

It is ideal to have a small sausage machine at home. They aren't that expensive and you can pick them up from any electrical goods store.

The machines help you mince the meat quickly as well as filling the cases consistently and quickly also.

We like to use fresh hog casings when making our snags at home. They are real intestines. You can ask your local butcher for some and they will come clean. They are easier to use and cook the best, leaving you with a crispy skin.

Take your time when making your very first batch of snags, you will appreciate it. We do like to also allow the fresh snags to sit in the fridge over night, which allows them to firm up and prevents them from splitting when cooking.

The best method of cooking sausages for us is under a hot grill.

HOMEMADE PORK SAUSAGES
WITH ONION GRAVY

SERVES 4-6

SAUSAGES
500 g/1 lb pork shoulder
375 g/13 oz pork back fat
250 g/9 oz skinless chicken thigh fillets
100 ml/3½ fl oz red wine
2 garlic cloves, chopped
2 teaspoons thyme, chopped
1 tablespoon salt
¼ teaspoon Chinese five spice
1 teaspoon ground black pepper
¼ teaspoon ground cumin
⅛ teaspoon cayenne pepper
½ cup parsley, chopped
1 tablespoon vegetable oil
natural sausage casings

Cut the pork shoulder, pork fat and chicken thighs into small enough sizes to push through the mincer.

Pass the pork fat through a 5 mm/¼ in mincer blade.

Then pass the pork shoulder and chicken thighs through a 10 mm/½ cm mincer blade.

Place both fat and meat together and pass through the 10 mm/½ cm blade together.

Place into a mixer with a dough hook. Add all the remaining seasonings, except the casings, to the meat and fat mixture.

Mix on a low speed to get a homogeneous mixture. Do not allow the fat to melt though as this will stiffen the mixture.

Set up the casings on the end of the sausage filling nozzle, pass the mixture through and fill the casings. This operation is to be done slowly and steady to avoid air pockets in your sausage.

If there are air pockets, prick with a toothpick and then smooth the sausage all over for a smooth surface.

Twist off into links after 10–12 cm/2 in long. Allow to sit and cool back in the fridge until needed for cooking.

Preheat a grill. Cut sausage links and place on a rack.

Place under a medium grill to cook, turning occasionally until evenly cooked and crispy.

To make the mash, place whole potatoes on an oiled oven tray and bake for 1 hour until soft.

ONION GRAVY

60 ml/2 fl oz olive oil

600 g/21 oz onions, sliced

1 tablespoon plain/all-purpose flour

100 ml/3½ fl oz red wine

500 ml/17½ fl oz beef stock

MASHED POTATO

1 kg/36 oz desiree potatoes

250 ml/9 fl oz cream, warmed

125 g/4 oz butter

salt and white pepper

fresh peas, podded

Peel potatoes and mash with a hand masher or through a ricer.

Add warm cream, butter and salt and pepper to taste. Mash and beat until smooth.

To make the onion gravy, heat olive oil in a medium saucepan and cook onions over medium heat for 15–20 minutes until golden brown.

Add the flour and cook, stirring for 1 minute. Add red wine and stir, scraping any caramelisation from the bottom of the pan until almost evaporated.

Add stock and simmer for 5–6 minutes until reduced and thick.

Blanch fresh peas for 1 minute.

To assemble, place a mound of mash on the plate, place 2 sausages on top of the mash, spoon on some peas, next to the sausages, then spoon over some onion gravy.

HOMEMADE PORK SAUSAGES WITH ONION GRAVY

BEEF SAUSAGES POACHED IN RED WINE
AND THYME WITH COLCANNON AND SMOKED HONEY CARROTS

SERVES 4

extra virgin olive oil
maldon salt
black pepper
fresh micro basil

SAUSAGES

1 kg/36 oz beef chuck,
partially frozen
300 g/10½ oz pork fat,
partially frozen
2 tablespoons mace
100–120 g/3½–4 oz
salt
60 g/2 oz white
pepper
fresh hog casings

SAUSAGE POACHING LIQUID

2 red onions, peeled
and sliced
1 tablespoon olive oil
½ bottle of red wine
4 sprigs of fresh
thyme, chopped
1 tablespoon tomato
puree
1 litre/2 pints salt-
reduced beef stock
1 teaspoon sugar

Using a mincer, pass the pork fat through a 5 mm/¼ in mincer blade. Then pass the beef through a 10 mm/½ in mincer blade.

Place both fat and meat together and pass through the 10 mm/½ in blade together. Mix together.

Dissolve the seasonings in a little water and then add this to the meat and fat mixture.

Mix together to get a homogeneous mixture, but do not allow the fat to melt as this will stiffen the mixture.

Using the sausage-filling nozzle, pass the mixture through and fill the casings. This operation is to be done slowly and steady to avoid air pockets in your sausage. If there are air pockets, prick with a toothpick and then smooth the sausage all over for a smooth surface.

Twist off into links, about 10–12 cm long—allow to sit and cool back in the fridge until needed for cooking.

Heat the olive oil in a large saucepan and gently cook the sausages and onions for at least 20 minutes or until the onions have turned gooey.

Add the red wine, thyme, tomato puree, beef stock and sugar. Give the mixture a stir and reduce over medium heat until the volume has halved.

Boil the potatoes in a pot of water until soft. While potatoes are boiling, heat cream, butter and sliced spring onions in a small saucepan.

Once potatoes are soft, drain and place back into a large pot.

Add the cream and butter mixture and mash and beat as much air in the potatoes as possible. Stir in the spring onions and kale. Season with salt and white pepper.

Steam the carrots until tender, but still slightly crisp. In a frying pan, add some butter and season with salt. Toss the carrots until they get some colouring on them.

COLCANNON

*8 Dutch cream
  potatoes, peeled and
  chopped*
*125–200 ml/4–7 fl oz
  cream*
*100 g/3½ oz unsalted
  butter*
*2–3 spring onions/
  scallions, finely sliced*
*100 g/3½ oz kale,
  blanched, finely
  chopped*
salt and white pepper

SMOKED HONEY CARROTS

*1–2 bunches of baby
  carrots, peeled*
smoking chips
2–4 tablespoons honey
salt and pepper

SAUCE

olive oil
1–2 tomatoes, diced
1 brown onion, diced
*leftover reduced
  sausage poaching
  liquid*

In a large baking tray, add 1–2 cups of smoking chips to one end and the other end add the carrots, piled up if necessary. Place foil over the tray and poke some holes in the foil above the carrots only.

Place this pan edge where the smoking chips are over a high flame and allow the chips to begin to smoke, you will start to see the smoke come out of the holes near the carrots.

Smoke for 2–3 minutes. After they've been smoked, drizzle some honey over the carrots and allow to sit until the honey has melted. Carefully toss so the carrots have been coated.

Slowly fry the tomato and onion in a pan until softened. Add some poaching liquid and reduce until a sauce consistency, season if necessary.

Ready to plate, add a generous amount of colcannon onto plate, sausages, carrots and then sauce, garnish with a sprinkling of micro basil.

VENISON SAUSAGE & LENTIL CASSEROLE

SAUSAGES
(MAKES 20)

500 g/1 lb pork back
    fat, minced
1.5 kg/3 lb 5 oz minced
    venison
150 ml/5 fl oz red wine
30 g/1 oz salt
2 teaspoons garlic,
    chopped
1 teaspoon black pepper
3 g fresh rosemary,
    finely chopped
3 g juniper berries,
    crushed
hog casings

CASSEROLE

1 tablespoon oil
8–10 venison sausages
150 g/5 oz pancetta,
    cubed
8 spring onions/
    scallions, cut in half
2 carrots, cut into
    chunks
8 garlic cloves, peeled
    and left whole
pinch of dried chilli
    flakes

This is amazing! But you have to know where to get venison. It isn't an everyday dish as venison is expensive.

Chop pork fat coarsely and mix through the venison mince.

Add the remaining sausage ingredients and mix well. Push the mixture through a sausage maker into the hog casings until you fill the entire hog case. Tie off and hang for as long as possible (24 hours would be ideal).

Make the brown chicken stock by roasting the chicken bones for 30 minutes in a hot oven at 250°C/480°F.

In a large stock pot, place the vegetables and herbs followed by the chicken carcasses. Top with cold water, covering all ingredients. Bring to the boil and then reduce the heat to barely simmer. Simmer uncovered for as long as possible, up to 4 hours would be sufficient

Remove bones, season with salt and pepper and strain stock.

Heat some oil in a large casserole pot. Add the sausages and brown them all over. Remove from the pan.

1 fresh rosemary sprig
2 fresh thyme sprigs
1 teaspoon tomato
  paste
250 g/9 oz green
  lentils
300 ml/10½ fl oz port
600 ml/21 fl oz
  chicken stock
1 teaspoon red currant
  jelly
½ a bunch parsley,
  roughly chopped

**BROWN CHICKEN
STOCK**
2 kg/4 lb 6.5 oz bones,
  skin and carcass
  from a deboned
  chicken
2 celery sticks
1 onion
2 carrots
½ bunch parsley
½ bunch thyme

Add pancetta to the same pan and cook for a couple of minutes. Add the spring onions, carrots and garlic cloves. Fry for 5 minutes until the pancetta becomes crispy and the vegetables have some colour. Add chilli flakes and herbs.

Add tomato paste and cook for 1 minute.

Stir in lentils, pour in port and chicken stock. Bring to the boil and then reduce to a simmer. Cover and simmer for 30 minutes until lentils have absorbed most of the liquid.

Stir in red currant jelly and sprinkle with chopped parsley.

SAUSAGE ROLLS

SERVES 4

500 g/1 lb pork mince
1 packet of good quality
  puff pastry
1 carrot, grated
1 onion, finely diced
2 eggs
parmesan cheese,
  grated
chilli flakes

Preheat the oven to 200°C/400°F, place all ingredients except 1 egg into a large bowl. Get your hands in there and give it a good mix up.

Your puff pastry will normally come in a big square. Slice it down the middle and place it onto a clean bench. Take the filling and spoon it all the way down the middle of your pastry rectangles, then roll them up.

Brush your sausage rolls with the egg wash then sprinkle over the parmesan cheese and chilli flakes.

Place sausage rolls into the preheated oven and bake for 25–30 minutes.

PASTA

MUSHROOM RAGU GNOCCHI

SERVES 4

GNOCCHI
750 g/24 oz brushed
   potatoes
200 g/7 oz plain/all-
   purpose flour
2 egg yolks
salt and cracked pepper
2 tablespoons butter
1 tablespoon olive oil

MUSHROOM RAGU
75 g/2½ oz butter
2 onions, finely diced
6 garlic cloves, sliced
¼ bunch of lemon
   thyme, finely
   chopped
salt and pepper
800 g/28 oz mixed
   mushrooms
   (Portobello, Swiss
   brown, field and
   oyster)

1 lemon, zest and juice,
   to serve
¼ bunch of parsley,
   finely chopped to
   serve
parmesan reggiano,
   shaved, to serve

Who doesn't like gnocchi? It's so easy to make and put with the right flavour can become a memorable dish.

Bake potatoes in the oven until soft. Peel potatoes and place in a large bowl. Add the flour and egg yolks and mash together to combine. Season to taste.

Knead the potato dough lightly and roll into logs, roughly 1.5 cm/½ in in diameter, then cut into 1.5 cm/1 in disks.

Bring a pot of salted water to the boil and add the gnocchi. Cook the gnocchi for about 2 minutes or until the gnocchi starts to float, remove and place onto paper towel to drain.

Melt butter in a large saucepan over a medium to high heat. Add onions, garlic, thyme and salt and pepper. Sweat the onions until softened.

Add the mushrooms to the pan and continue cooking until softened. Remove from the pan and set aside.

Heat oil and butter in the same saucepan. Add gnocchi and pan-fry until golden brown. Add back in the mushroom ragu and heat through.

Plate good spoonfuls of gnocchi onto the centre of the plate, stacking high, finish with lemon zest, lemon juice, chopped parsley and shaved reggiano.

FRIED GNOCCHI
WITH BLUE CHEESE SAUCE

SERVES 4

GNOCCHI
750 g/ brushed
  potatoes
200 g/ plain/all-
  purpose flour
2 egg yolks
salt and cracked pepper

**BLUE CHEESE
SAUCE**
1 cup whipping cream
3 cups crumbled
  gorgonzola cheese

fresh chives, chopped,
  for serving
parmesan cheese,
  grated, for serving

Bake potatoes in the oven until soft. Peel potatoes and place in a large bowl. Add flour and egg yolks and mash to combine. Season to taste.

Knead the potato dough lightly and roll into logs, roughly 1.5 cm/½ in in diameter, then cut into 1.5 cm/½ in disks.

Bring a pot of salted water to the boil and add the gnocchi. Cook for 2 minutes or until they start to float. Remove and place onto paper towel to drain.

In a large frying pan, heat the olive oil over a medium to high heat. Add the gnocchi and fry until golden and remove from heat.

Bring cream to a simmer in a heavy medium-sized saucepan over medium heat.

Add gorgonzola, whisking until melted. Spoon sauce over gnocchi. Sprinkle with chives and parmesan.

Serve while still warm.

MUSHROOM RAGU, FRESH PAPPARDELLE
AND THYME

SERVES 4

1 quantity Pasta Dough
  (see recipe, p. 18)

600 g/21 oz button or
  mixed mushrooms
2 tablespoons unsalted
  butter
1 tablespoon coarse
  milled black pepper
½ tablespoon salt
1 tablespoon dried
  thyme
¼–½ cup cream
1/3 bunch of fresh
  parsley
fresh thyme, to serve
parmesan, shaved, to
  serve

In a large frying pan, cook the mushrooms, butter, pepper, salt and thyme into a pot and cook down until the mushrooms are soft. Stir in the cream and parsley and heat through, season to taste.

Bring a big pot of salted water to the boil and cook the pasta and cook for a few minutes until al dente.

Stir through the mushroom ragu with pasta and top with shaved parmesan and fresh thyme leaves.

BALINESE SNAPPER

SERVES 4

CURRY PASTE
6 garlic cloves
6 spring onions/
　scallions
6 red chillies
　(3 deseeded)
4 stalks of lemongrass,
　finely sliced
2 tomatoes, chopped
4 cm/2 in knob of
　ginger, grated
4 cm/2 in knob of
　galangal, grated
8 macadamia nuts
4 coriander stems and
　roots, finely sliced
pinch of nutmeg
1 teaspoon shrimp
　paste
2 teaspoons tamarind
　puree
3 tablespoons palm
　sugar, to taste
2 tablespoons turmeric
　powder

Firstly, make the curry paste. Place all ingredients into a food processor and blend until it forms a paste. Add more water and oil to the spices if they won't blend in the food processor, or pound in a mortar and pestle until a paste forms and all the ingredients are soft.

Heat a little peanut oil in a saucepan over a medium heat and add the curry paste, cook the paste for 2–3 minutes, until fragrant and glossy, stirring constantly.

Season to taste with salt and pepper.

In a large saucepan, place coconut oil, kaffir lime leaves, lemongrass, ginger and bay leaves and stir frequently while heating until very fragrant, reduce heat to medium and add 4 to 5 tablespoons of curry paste and cook stirring occasionally until very fragrant and for about 4 minutes. Leave the lemongrass, ginger and bay leaves in the pot.

Pour in the coconut milk and stir, allow to simmer away for 5 minutes, then reduce heat to a very low simmer and add snapper fillets.

Poach the fillets in the curry paste for 5 to 6 minutes, or until opaque in colour and cooked through. Carfeully remove fillets from curry and then drain the curry sauce keeping the liquid for dressing at time of serving.

2 tablespoons peanut
oil

salt and pepper, to
season

80 ml/2½ fl oz coconut
oil

3 kaffir lime leaves

2 stalks of lemongrass,
bruised

2 cm/1 in knob of
ginger, sliced

2 bay leaf

1 x 440 ml/15 fl oz tin
of coconut milk

4 large snapper fillets

2 cups jasmine rice,
uncooked

1 chilli, deseeded and
finely sliced, to serve

coriander/cilantro
leaves, to serve

4 lime cheeks, to serve

Bring a large pot of water to the boil. Wash your rice in a sieve until the water runs clear.

Once the water has boiled, add rice and cover with a lid. Bring to a boil again then reduce heat to a simmer, leaving the lid on the pot. Set timer for 15 minutes.

After 15 minutes, turn off the heat and allow your rice to steam for 10 minutes, do not take the lid off the pot.

Take the lid off and fluff the rice with a fork.

To serve in a bowl place a mound of rice, top with a fillet of fish and then spoon over some delicious curry sauce.

Top with fresh chilli, coriander and a cheek of lime.

BALINESE SNAPPER

CRISPY SKIN FISH WITH
TAMARIND AND CUCUMBER PICKLE

SERVES 4

180 g/6 oz flat rice
   noodles
4 x 200 g/7 oz pieces
   white flesh fish, skin
   left on
2–4 tablespoons olive
   oil
coriander/cilantro
   leaves, for garnish
red chilli, finely sliced
   into rings for garnish
80 g/2½ oz peanuts

CUCUMBER
PICKLE

1 red onion, thinly
   sliced
1 teaspoon caster/
   superfine sugar
1 teaspoon white wine
   vinegar
2 teaspoons red wine
   vinegar
80 ml/2½ fl oz
   grapeseed oil
2 Lebanese cucumbers,
   ribboned
60 ml/2 fl oz tamarind
   puree
¼ teaspoon white
   pepper

Make the cucumber pickle by placing the onion in a bowl and adding the sugar and a pinch of salt. Stir to separate the onion slices. Leave for 15 minutes for onion to soften.

Whisk the vinegars together with 2 tablespoons of grapeseed oil and stir to combine.

Stir in ribboned cucumber, tamarind puree, white pepper and onion. Set aside.

Soak the flat rice noodles in boiling water for 5 minutes, until soft.

In a large frying pan, over high heat, add oil.

Season the fish skin with salt and score the skin slightly.

Once the pan is smoking hot, add the fish, skin side down, pressing down on the flesh so that the skin does not curl up. Cook for 4 minutes until the skin is crispy. Turn and cook for a further 3 minutes until cooked through. Remove from the pan and place on a paper towel.

To serve, place a small mound of rice noodles on the plate. Top with a serving of the pickle, a piece of fish and garnish with coriander leaves, sliced chilli and peanuts on each plate.

SMOKED SALMON, PEA AND
RADISH SALAD, PRESERVED LEMON, MINTED YOGHURT

SERVES 4

*400 g/14 oz smoked
  salmon*
*2 cups frozen peas,
  defrosted*
*1 bunch of radish,
  thinly sliced*
watercress, picked
*2–3 preserved lemons,
  sliced very thin and
  only a few slices*
dill, to serve

MINTED YOGHURT

*250 ml/9 fl oz Greek
  yoghurt*
*1 bunch of fresh mint,
  finely chopped*
juice of ½ lemon
pinch of salt

Combine all the minted yoghurt ingredients together.

Arrange all of the salad ingredients on a large platter or plate. Season lightly with a drizzle of olive oil and salt and pepper. Dollop the minted yoghurt over the top.

GRILLED BBQ SHRIMP,
FENNEL AND GRAPEFRUIT SALAD AND TOASTED QUINOA

SERVES 4

SHRIMP/PRAWN MARINADE

4 tablespoons olive oil

4 tablespoons lemon juice

3 tablespoons fresh parsley, chopped

1 tablespoon minced garlic

freshly ground black pepper to taste

700 g/1 lb 9 oz uncooked fresh king prawns/shrimp, peeled and deveined

In a large bowl, stir together the olive oil, lemon juice, parsley, garlic and black pepper.

Add prawns and toss to coat. Marinate in the refrigerator for 30 minutes.

Preheat the barbecue to a high heat. Thread prawns onto skewers, piercing once near the tail and once near the head. Discard any remaining marinade.

Lightly oil the barbecue grill or hotplate. Cook for 2 to 3 minutes per side, or until opaque.

In a small jar with a tight-fitting lid, combine all of the vinaigrette ingredients. Shake vigorously, to emulsify the dressing.

Trim the fennel bulb by cutting across the top to remove the stalks (save the green fronds), and slicing across the bottom at the root end. Cut the bulb in half lengthwise, and remove the hard core from each half.

Use a mandolin slicer, if you have one, to create paper-thin slices of fennel. Or, slice as thinly as you can with a very sharp knife.

Peel the avocado and cut into slices. Add them to a bowl with the fennel and grapefruit segments. Add in chopped snow pea sprouts.

Recipe cont.

GRILLED BBQ SHRIMP
CONT.

VINAIGRETTE

*juice of ½ orange
(approximately 2
teaspoons)*

*1 teaspoon wholegrain
mustard (or use what
you have)*

*pinch of salt and black
pepper*

*2 teaspoons extra
virgin olive oil*

**GRAPEFRUIT AND
FENNEL SALAD**

*1 large fennel bulb,
trimmed and thinly
sliced*

1 ripe avocado

*1 cup grapefruit
segments*

*1 bunch of pea sprouts,
chopped in half*

TOASTED QUINOA

1 cup quinoa
water (for cleaning)

Immediately toss with the vinaigrette, making sure to distribute the dressing over all of the avocado and fennel.

Just before serving, toss some of the green fennel fronds into the salad.

Soak quinoa in water for up to 5 minutes and then rinse under water until it runs clear. Allow to drain.

Coat a frying pan with olive oil spray and heat over a high heat. Swish the soaked quinoa around the pan, it will begin to dry out and pop, there will be a nutty aroma coming from it. Once it begins to toast and brown slightly it is ready—allow to cool before sprinkling onto salad at the time of serving.

SCALLOP CEVICHE
AND CORN SALSA

SERVES 4

micro coriander/
* cilantro leaves*

SCALLOPS
20 Hervey Bay
* scallops, out of shell*
juice of 2–3 limes

CORN SALSA
1 corn cobs, boiled
1 corn cobs, char-
* grilled*
¼ red onion, finely
* diced*
½ red capsicum/bell
* pepper, finely diced*
1 tablespoon honey
¼ bunch of chives,
* finely diced*

AVOCADO PUREE
1 avocado
1 tablespoon olive oil
juice of ½ lime
a few drops of tabasco
* sauce*
salt and pepper

Boil the corn and char-grill the corn under the grill. Allow to cool and then cut the kernels off.

Soak the red onion in water for up to 5 minutes.

Mix capsicum, onion, corn, chives, honey. Season with salt and pepper.

Puree the avocado, olive oil and lime juice in a food processor or a blender until smooth. Season with salt and pepper to taste if necessary and tabasco to taste.

Prior to plating, add the scallop to the lime juice and allow to be marinated for 4 minutes.

Strain from juice and plate immediately. Each plate will have 5 scallops. Brush a tablespoon of avocado puree onto plate, then place on 5 scallops. Sprinkle the corn salsa around and dollop on some avocado puree. Finish with baby coriander on top and a small sprinkling of salt.

SALT AND PEPPER SQUID
WITH ASIAN SALAD

SERVES 4

60 g/2 oz sea salt
½ teaspoon Sichuan
  pepper
1 star anise
1 cinnamon stick
600 g/21 oz squid,
  sliced into strips
160–320 g/5½–11 oz
  rice flour
vegetable oil, for frying
4 lemon wedges

**WASABI
MAYONNAISE**

3 egg yolks
2 tablespoons of white
  wine vinegar
200 ml/7 fl oz
  grapeseed oil
salt and white pepper
  to taste
1–2 teaspoons wasabi
  paste

ASIAN SALAD

rocket leaves
mint leaves
coriander/cilantro leaves
bean sprouts
1–2 long red chillies,
  chopped into thin
  slices

DRESSING

2 spring onions/
  scallions, finely sliced
1 tablespoon rice
  vinegar
1 teaspoon sugar
2 tablespoons extra
  virgin olive oil
1 tablespoon mirin
1 teaspoon toasted
  sesame oil
salt and pepper, to taste

In a hot frying pan, fry the salt, Sichuan pepper, star anise and cinnamon and cook for about 2 minutes until just smoking and the flavours are very fragrant.

Place these ingredients into a small food processor and blend until well combined. Set aside for dusting the squid.

Pat the squid dry and cut into strips. Place all squid pieces into a freezer bag with the rice flour. Toss to coat all pieces and then shake off any excess.

Heat oil in a large saucepan until hot.

Add the squid pieces and cook for 2 to 3 minutes. The pieces should be golden and crisp.

Transfer the pieces to some paper towel to drain and then place into a big bowl.

Sprinkle the pieces with the salt and pepper spice mix, then toss to coat.

To make the Asian salad, carefully pick the salad leaves and place into a large bowl. Make the salad dressing by combining all ingredients together and mixing well. Dress the salad well.

Serve the squid with the salad and wasabi mayonnaise for dipping.

SWEETS

CHOCOLATE MOUSSE

SERVES 4

50 g/1¾ oz unsalted
  butter
240 g/8½ oz 70%
  cocoa dark chocolate
4 eggs, separated
90 g/3 oz caster/
  superfine sugar
240 ml/8½ fl oz
  whipping cream
4 egg whites
150 g/5 oz caster/
  superfine sugar
60 ml/2 oz water
4 fresh cherries, for
  garnish
½ cup shredded
  coconut, toasted for
  garnish

Half-fill a large pot with water. Bring to the boil and then reduce heat to a low simmer—place a metal or glass bowl over the pot and add the butter and chocolate.

Melt butter and chocolate until the chocolate has reached 57°C/134°F on a candy thermometer. Remove from the heat and keep the bowl over the water bath until needed.

In another saucepan, bring a small amount of water to the boil, then reduce to a low simmer.

In a heatproof bowl, add the egg yolks and sugar and whisk together. Place this bowl of eggs over the simmering water and whisk until the yolk mixture reaches at least 74°C/165°F.

Remove from heat and continue to whip until the mixture is lukewarm or 35°C/95°F.

Whip the cream until soft peaks form. Set aside.

Place egg whites in a clean dry bowl.

In a small saucepan, add the second lot of sugar and the water and bring to the boil. Once boiling, brush the inside of the pan with a wet brush to remove any crystallisation.

Continue to boil without stirring until it is just about to reach 118°C/245°F. Just before it reaches that temperature, start whipping the egg whites at a medium speed.

Once the syrup has reached the temperature, remove from heat and immediately pour it into the egg white bowl, but not directly, pour it along the edges of the bowl.

Whip until meringue reaches 30°C/86°F and then stop whipping.

Recheck the temperature of the melted chocolate—if it is not at 57°C/134°F, reheat.

Add ¼ of the whipped cream to the chocolate and whisk into a ganache. Add and fold in the creamed yolk and sugar mixture. Add the meringue mixture in increments (rewhip the meringue just before adding) or do it very quickly.

Then gently fold in the remaining whipped cream and immediately place into the fridge.

Serve garnished with fresh cherries and toasted coconut. This mousse is unbelievably delicious and airy!

PASSIONFRUIT AND LEMON TART
WITH COCONUT DOUBLE CREAM

PASTRY

125 g/4 oz cold
  unsalted butter
250 g/9 oz plain/all-
  purpose flour
75 g/2½ oz icing/
  confectioner's sugar
  plus extra for dusting
3 egg yolks
iced water

FILLING

5 eggs
150 g/5 oz caster/
  superfine sugar
70 ml/2½ fl oz
  passionfruit juice, no
  pips
20 ml/²/3 fl oz lemon
  juice
zest of 2 lemons

TO SERVE

1 cup double cream
½ cup coconut cream
passionfruit pulp, for
  serving

Process butter, flour and icing sugar in a processor until it forms crumbs.

Add egg yolks one at a time followed by the iced water until the mixture comes together in one big ball in the processor.

Turn onto a floured surface and lightly knead the dough together. Wrap the dough in cling wrap and rest in the fridge for 30 minutes.

Oil a rectangular fluted 35 cm x 13 cm pan with a removable bottom.

Roll out the rested pastry, to the mentioned thickness to the shape of the fluted pan. You will have excess pastry but once you have placed the pastry in the pan, you can trim the edges to fit. Gently place the pastry into the pan, pressing the pastry into the edges and corners. Prick the bottom with a fork a few times. Place back in the refrigerator for a further 30 minutes.

Preheat the oven to 160°C/320°F. Line the pastry with baking paper and fill with baking weights or dried beans or rice. Blind bake for 10–12 minutes.

Remove the beans and paper and bake for a further 15 minutes until golden brown.

Place the eggs, sugar, lemon juice, passionfruit juice, lemon zest in a bowl and whisk to combine. Allow to infuse for at least 30 minutes.

Whisk in the cream, then pour the mixture into a saucepan and heat on low for 5 minutes. Pour into the pastry case.

Bake in the oven for 25 minutes at the same temperature. The tart should be just firm and have a slight wobble to it. Allow to cool before placing back in the refrigerator.

Whisk the double cream until almost thick, then add coconut cream and whisk further until thick.

To serve, cut a nice slice of tart and serve with a quenelle of coconut cream, drizzle cream with some fresh passionfruit pulp with seeds and dust the tart with icing sugar.

Notes
Once the pastry case has been blind baked, if the pastry edges are uneven, before pouring in the filling, trim the edges of the inside of the case so it is even all around.

At the end of baking, wiggle the case a little and the filling should have a slight wobble to it; over cooking will make the filling crack.

MANGO RASPBERRY TART

SERVES 4

CRUST

4 cups mixed nuts
(macadamias,
almonds and walnuts)
1 cup pitted packed
dates

FILLING

4 cups diced fresh
mango
4 tablespoons coconut
oil
3 cups cashews
½ cup honey
3–4 tablespoons lemon
juice
1–2 gelatin leaves
²/3 cup cacao butter
3 cups fresh
raspberries

Firstly, make the crust by processing the nuts and dates together in a food processor.

Add 1–2 teaspoons of water, if the mixture is too dry and crumbly. It should combine together when pressed. Press the mixture into 4 mini tart pans.

Make the filling by blending the mango, coconut oil, cashews, honey and lemon juice until smooth and creamy.

Soak the gelatin leaves in water until soft.

Add the cacao butter to the mango mixture slowly until completely mixed.

Squeeze the softened gelatin and blend it into the mango mixture.

Evenly spread some of the raspberries over the crust and then smash them down with a fork.

Pour the mango filling over the top.

Chill the tart in the fridge until the filling has set. Just before serving, garnish with the fresh raspberries on top of the tart and dust with some icing sugar.

MINI PAVLOVAS

SERVES 20

MINI MERINGUES
6 egg whites
1½ cups caster/
*   superfine sugar*

LEMON CURD
6 eggs
6 egg yolks
450 g/15 oz caster/
*   superfine sugar*
240 g/8½ oz unsalted
*   butter, chilled*
zest of 4–6 lemons
juice of 8–10 lemons

FILLING
200 g/7 oz pistachios,
*   for garnish*
1 kg/2 lb 4 oz fresh
*   strawberries, diced*
1 large bunch of mint
*   leaves, finely chopped*
800 ml/28 fl oz
*   whipping cream*
1 vanilla bean, seeds
*   only*
zest of 2 lemons, for
*   garnish*

Preheat the oven to 150°C/300°F. Spread the pistachios onto a greased or lined baking tray. Toast the nuts in the oven for 5–10 minutes. Keep a close eye on them, then remove and cool. Leave the oven on.

Once cooled, place the nuts in a food processor and process quickly to make a crumb. The crumb doesn't have to be all the same size, you want a rustic look. These will be sprinkled on top of the pavlova at the time of serving.

Place the egg whites into a clean dry bowl and whisk with electric beaters until soft peaks form. Gradually add the sugar to the egg whites, a small amount at a time.

Continue this process until all the sugar is added and dissolved. Continue to beat mixture until it is thick and glossy.

Transfer the mixture to a piping bag, with a medium nozzle. Pipe the mixture onto the baking paper, following the circles that you may have drawn and create a meringue cup. Bake in the oven for 20–25 minutes or until crisp.

Turn the oven off, leave the door ajar and leave the pavlovas in the oven to cool completely—they will crisp up.

Make the lemon curd, by whisking the eggs, egg yolks and sugar in a saucepan until smooth. Place the saucepan over a low heat and then add the butter, zest and juice. Whisk continuously until thickened.

Strain through a fine sieve, cover and refrigerate until cool.

Whip the cream and vanilla bean seeds together until soft peaks form. Transfer into a piping bag with a medium round nozzle and place back in the fridge until you are ready to assemble.

To assemble the pavlova's, spoon curd into each shell, top with strawberries, mint, cream and then sprinkle with pistachios. Serve immediately.

Notes
To pipe perfect circles, draw circles onto the baking paper first. You can create a meringue cup by piping the bottom in a spiral motion first, then piping around the edges in a circular motion so the edges come up higher than the middle, allowing room to hold the fillings.

Or you can spoon mixture onto the paper and flatten out with the back of a spoon for a more rustic look.

GINGER AND PEAR CAKE

SERVES 4

225 g/8 oz butter,
  softened

250 g/9 oz dark brown
  sugar

4 Bosch pears, cut
  into 8 wedges, core
  removed

450 g/15 oz all-
  purpose/plain flour,
  sifted

1 teaspoon baking
  soda/bicarbonate of
  soda

3 tablespoons ground
  ginger

1½ teaspoons ground
  cinnamon

1 teaspoon ground
  nutmeg

370 g/13 oz treacle

50 g/1¾ oz fresh
  ginger, grated

3 eggs

250 ml/9 fl oz
  buttermilk

200 g/7 oz pecans

300 ml/10½ fl oz
  thickened cream, for
  serving

½–1 teaspoon vanilla
  extract

Preheat the oven to 160°C/320°F and grease and line a 22 cm/8 in round cake tin.

In a large frying pan, over medium heat, melt 100 g/3½ oz of the butter, then scatter over half the sugar and stir to dissolve.

Add the pears and cook until golden and just cooked all the way through, turning occasionally.

Remove from the pan and arrange the pear wedges into the bottom of the cake tin. Set aside, but reserve the liquid in the frying pan.

Sift the flour, baking soda and spices into a bowl and set aside.

Beat the rest of the butter and remaining sugar until pale and creamy. Add the vanilla.

Beat in the treacle until combined, add the grated ginger and then the eggs, one at a time—be sure to beat well after each addition.

Turn the mixer to a low speed and gradually add the flour mixture, a little at a time, alternating with the buttermilk. Be sure to finish with the flour and whisk slowly until just combined. Stir in the pecans. Pour the mixture over the pears in the cake tin.

Place into the oven for 50 minutes or until a skewer comes out clean when inserted.

Cool in cake tin for 10 minutes and then invert onto a plate.

Heat the reserved juices in the pan and whisk in the cream to make a caramel—pour this over the cake as it is cooling.

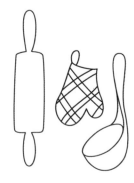

CHOCOLATE BROWNIE

MAKES ABOUT 12

180 g/6 oz unsalted
  butter
180 g/6 oz dark
  chocolate
3 eggs
250 g/9 oz caster/
  superfine sugar
1 teaspoon vanilla paste
110 g/3½ oz plain/all-
  purpose flour, sifted
pinch of salt

**FLAVOUR
VARIATIONS**

1 cup raspberries OR
1 cup blueberries and
  white choc chips OR
2 tablespoons orange
  marmalade OR
smoked salt, to taste

Preheat the oven to 180°C/350°F. Grease and line a rectangular baking tray.
  Melt butter and chocolate together in a saucepan over a low heat.
  In a bowl, whisk eggs, sugar and vanilla together until light, fluffy and doubled in size. Add salt.
  Add half of the flour to egg mixture and then half of the chocolate mixture and combine. Add in the remaining flour and then the remaining chocolate and combine all of the ingredients. If adding in any particular flavours, add them to the brownie mixture now.
  Pour into the lined tray and bake for 20–25 minutes.
  Remove and allow to cool.

MERINGUE WITH PASSIONFRUIT CURD,
MANGO AND WHIPPED COCONUT CREAM

SERVES 4

**PASSIONFRUIT
CURD**
11 passionfruit, pulped
2 eggs
2 egg yolks
*150 g/5 oz caster/
   superfine sugar*
*100 g/3½ oz unsalted
   butter*

MERINGUE
*(makes about 36 mini
   meringues)*
½ cup macadamia nuts
3 egg whites
*¾ cup caster/superfine
   sugar*
*½ teaspoon white
   vinegar*
*1 teaspoon vanilla
   extract*
*1 teaspoon cornflour/
   cornstarch*

You will need bamboo skewers, a piece of polystyrene and one sheet of newspaper for this recipe.

To make the passionfruit curd, put the pulps of 10 passionfruit into a processor and blitz until the seeds are loose. Strain the mixture and reserve the liquid and the pulp.

Beat the eggs, yolks and sugar together until thick and pale.

Melt the butter over a low heat and, once melted, gradually stir in the egg mixture then the passionfruit juice. Continue to cook on low heat, stirring constantly until the mixture thickens.

Off the heat, stir thought the pulp and remaining passionfruit, place in a jar and place in the fridge.

To make coconut cream, place the coconut milk can into the fridge overnight, this will allow it to separate.

Once cold, flip the can over and pour out the clear liquid. Scoop the solid white cream into a bowl. Add the icing sugar and whip until soft peaks form. Add the vanilla seeds and stir through. Place the cream into the fridge to firm back up.

Recipe cont.

MERINGUE WITH PASSIONFRUIT CURD
CONT.

WHIPPED COCONUT CREAM

1 x 400 ml/14 fl oz can coconut milk

1 tablespoon icing/confectioner's sugar

1 vanilla bean, seeds only

CANDIED MACADAMIAS

12 whole macadamia nuts

1 cup caster/superfine sugar

2 tablespoons water

3 fresh mangoes

2 limes

micro mint

Preheat the oven to 200°C/400°F.

Place macadamia nuts on a baking tray in a hot oven and toast until slightly browned and fragrant. This won't take long, so keep an eye on them. Remove the nuts and allow to cool before roughly crushing them.

Lower the temperature of the oven to 120°C/250°F. Line 2 baking trays with paper and draw circles on it, depending on what size you want the meringues.

Place the egg whites into a clean dry bowl and whisk with electric beaters until soft peaks form. Gradually add the sugar to the egg whites, a small amount at a time.

Continue beating until all the sugar has been combined. Beat in the vinegar. Add in the cornflour and vanilla and beat until stiff peaks form and the mixture is glossy.

Spoon into a piping bag and pipe into the circles you've drawn on the prepared trays. Bake in the oven for 20–30 minutes, until a slight colour appears

Turn off the oven, leave the oven door ajar and leave meringues in there until completely cool.

To make candied macadamia nuts, skewer each nut, ready for dipping. Set up your polystyrene with the newspaper spread out underneath—you want to be able to stick the dipped nut/skewer into it and allow the candy to drip off.

Add the sugar and water in a saucepan over a high heat. Wipe the sides of the saucepan with a wet brush, preventing the syrup from crystallising on the sides.

RASPBERRY & WHITE CHOCOLATE
MUFFINS

MAKES ABOUT 12

*2 cups plain/all-
purpose flour*
*2 teaspoons baking
powder*
*1 cup caster/superfine
sugar*
1 egg
1 cup milk
*50 g/1¾ oz butter,
melted*
*1 cup frozen
raspberries, thawed*
*200 g/7 oz white
chocolate, roughly
chopped*

Preheat the oven to 180°C/350°F.

Grease and line a baking tray with paper cup muffin liners.

Sift the flour and baking powder into the same bowl. Add in the sugar.

In another bowl, whisk together the egg, milk and butter.

Add wet ingredients to dry and then fold in the raspberries and chocolate using a wooden spoon.

Put in patties and bake for 20–25 minutes until golden.

RAW BANANA AND DATE SLICE

MAKES ABOUT 12 SLICES

BASE

1 cup cashews or almonds or a mix of nuts
¾ cup desiccated coconut
1 cup dried pitted dates
pinch of salt

TOPPING

2 bananas, slightly over-ripe
½ cup cashews
¼ cup almonds
¼ cup honey
¼ cup lemon juice
1/3 cup coconut oil
1 teaspoon vanilla paste
pinch of salt

Firstly, line a rectangular tray with baking paper.

In a processor, blitz nuts, coconut, dates and salt together until fine and the mixture sticks together when touched.

Place the base mixture into your tray and press firmly, spreading the base evenly over the bottom of tray. Place the tray in the fridge to firm up while you make the topping.

Put all of the topping ingredients into a processor and blitz until smooth.

Pour mixture over the refrigerated base and smooth out. Place the tray back into the fridge overnight to firm.

Slice and serve when set.

HAZELNUT MERINGUE WITH BERRIES
AND CHOCOLATE SAUCE

HAZELNUT MERINGUE

3 egg whites

150 g/5 oz caster/ superfine sugar

1 tablespoons cornflour/cornstarch

50 g/1¾ oz hazelnuts, some roughly chopped, some finely chopped

MASCARPONE TOPPING

250 g/9 oz mascarpone

150 ml/5 fl oz strawberry yoghurt

CHOCOLATE SAUCE

1 cup water

½ cup caster/superfine sugar

½ cup glucose syrup

¾ cup unsweetened cocoa powder

55 g/2 oz bittersweet chocolate, finely chopped

fresh strawberries, thickly sliced

60 g/2 oz hazelnuts, toasted and roughly chopped

zest of 1 orange

Preheat the oven to 200°C/400°F. Place a flat baking tray into the oven to heat through for 19 minutes, this assures a crisp base to your meringue.

Whisk egg whites using electric beaters on a high speed until soft peaks form, then gradually sprinkle in the sugar and cornflour. Whisk on high until stiff peaks form. Gently fold in hazelnuts.

Place baking paper onto the warm tray and using a large spoon, dollop the mixture into 5 cm/2½ in high mounds. Allow room to spread while cooking.

Reduce the oven to 180°C/350°F and place the tray in oven for 20–25 minutes, turn off the oven and open door just slightly and allow to cool in oven, then remove to cool completely.

For the topping, beat the mascarpone and strawberry yoghurt together until it forms soft peaks.

While the meringue is cooling, make the chocolate sauce by putting the water, sugar, glucose syrup and cocoa powder in a saucepan over a medium heat. Bring the mixture to a simmer and almost boil, then remove from the heat, stir in the chopped chocolate and stir until melted. Allow to stand for an hour before serving, as it will thicken.

To serve, place the large meringue on a wooden board, dollop on the mascarpone topping, push in some fresh strawberries, drizzle over chocolate sauce and sprinkle with some toasted hazelnuts and some orange zest.

SMOKED MERINGUE
WITH POACHED APPLES,
CINNAMON CREAM AND SALTED CARAMEL WALNUT PRALINE

SERVES 4

MERINGUE
3 egg whites
150 g/5 oz caster/
*   superfine sugar*
1 tablespoon cornflour/
*   cornstarch*
1 teaspoon vanilla
*   extract or 1 vanilla*
*   bean, seeds only*

**SALTED CARAMEL
PRALINE**
50 g/1¾ oz brown
*   sugar*
50 g/1¾ oz caster/
*   superfine sugar*
50 g/1¾ oz golden
*   syrup*
20 ml/⅔ fl oz cream
1 teaspoon salt flakes
80 g/2½ oz walnuts,
*   chopped*
fresh thyme or micro
*   mint, for garnish*

To make a smoked meringue, we use a Bradley Smoker. If you don't have a smoke oven, refer to the instructions below.

Preheat the smoke oven to 110–120°C/230–250°F.

Place baking paper onto a rack.

Place the egg whites into a clean dry bowl and whisk with electric beaters until soft peaks form. Gradually add the sugar to the egg whites, a small amount at a time.

Continue this process until all the sugar has been added and dissolved.

Add the cornflour and vanilla extract or vanilla bean seeds. Continue to beat the mixture until it is thick and glossy.

Transfer the mixture to a piping bag, with a medium nozzle. Pipe small dollops of the mixture onto the baking paper.

Bake the meringues in the smoke oven for 30–40 minutes or until crispy. Once meringues are crispy, turn off smoker, leave the oven door ajar and allow to cool completely in the smoker.

If you don't have a smoke oven, cook the meringues in a 130°C/265°F oven for 40 minutes or until crispy. Once they are cooked, simply use an old baking dish and place some smoking chips on the bottom, place a wire rack on top and place the meringues on there, tightly cover with foil and poke 4 holes in the foil. Over a high heat on the stove top, heat up the baking dish with smoking chips and allow to smoke.

To make salted caramel praline, place the sugars and golden syrup into a saucepan with a dash of water and allow to melt over a medium–high heat. Simmer for 4 minutes, swirling to continue melting the mixture.

Once the praline reaches 110°C/230°F on a candy thermometer, slowly and carefully pour in cream, swirling the saucepan to combine.

Bring the temperature to around 130–140°C/265–285°F. Once reached, put the bottom of the saucepan in cold water until it stops sizzling.

Pour out onto a silicone mat and sprinkle over the chopped walnuts and salt. Allow to cool completely.

To make the poached apples, place the water, wine, ginger and cinnamon stick into a large saucepan and bring to the boil.

POACHED APPLES

2 cups water
1 cup sweet dessert wine
2 cm/1 in piece fresh ginger, peeled and sliced
½ cinnamon stick
2 Granny Smith apples, balled

CINNAMON CREAM

7 fl oz/200 ml thickened cream
1–2 tablespoon ground cinnamon

Reduce heat to a simmer and place in the apple balls. Make a cartouche by cutting a circle of baking paper that will fit just inside the saucepan. Place this over the apples to keep them submerged as they are poached.

Poach for 5–8 minutes until tender. Remove from the liquid and allow to cool.

Make the cinnamon cream by whisking the thickened cream and ground cinnamon together. Whisk until very thick.

To serve, spread some cinnamon cream onto each plate, place 5 meringues on the cream, then place on the poached apples. Scatter over the praline.

Notes
To pipe perfect circles, draw circles onto the baking paper first. You can create a meringue cup by piping the bottom in a spiral motion first, then piping around the edges in a circular motion so the edges come up higher than the middle, allowing room to hold the fillings.
Or you can spoon mixture onto the paper and flatten out with the back of a spoon for a more rustic look.

DATE LOAF

MAKES 1 LOAF

1½ cups dates
1 cup water
1 teaspoon ground
  mixed spice
1 cup brown sugar,
  packed
60 g/2 oz unsalted
  butter
1¾ cups self-raising/
  self-rising flour,
  sifted
1 teaspoon bicarbonate
  of soda/baking soda
2 teaspoons vanilla
  extract

Preheat the oven to 180°C/350°F. Grease and line a loaf tin.

Roughly chop the dates. In a saucepan, add the dates, water, mixed spice, sugar and butter. On a high heat, bring the mixture to the boil and allow the sugar to dissolve and the butter completely melt.

In a bowl, sift the self-rising flour and bicarbonate of soda.

Once the sugar is dissolved and the butter has melted, pour the wet ingredients over the flour and add vanilla.

Stir with a wooden spoon until all combined.

Pour into a loaf tin and bake for 40–45 minutes. Serve warm with salted butter.

SPICED RHUBARB CRUMBLE AND
CRÈME ANGLAISE

RHUBARB

whole star anise (to
make ½ teaspoon
ground star anise)
14 oz/400 g rhubarb
stalks
½ teaspoon ground
ginger
5 oz/150 g caster/
superfine sugar
juice of ½ blood orange
zest of 1 blood orange

CRUMBLE

5 oz/150 g plain/all-
purpose flour
5 oz/150 g unsalted
butter
3½ oz/100 g porridge
oats
3½ oz/100 g almonds,
crushed
3½ oz/100 g raw/
demerara sugar
½ teaspoon ground
cinnamon

SPICED CRÈME
ANGLAISE

9 fl oz/250 ml milk
9 fl oz/250 ml cream
1 vanilla bean, cut
in half and seeds
scraped out

5 egg yolks
3½ oz/100 g caster/
superfine sugar
1–2 teaspoon ground
cardamom
2 blood oranges,
segmented, to serve

Preheat the oven to 180°C/350°F.

To make the rhubarb, toast the whole star anise in a frying pan until smoking, then ground them using a mortar and pestle.

Place the rhubarb, ginger, star anise, caster sugar, orange juice and orange zest into a saucepan and cook gently, uncovered, until just soft. Cool a little and then spoon into an ovenproof baking dish.

To make the crumble, rub the flour and butter together until the mixture resembles breadcrumbs.

Stir in the oats, nuts, sugar and cinnamon. Spoon the crumble on top of the rhubarb.

Bake in the oven for 20–30 minutes, or until the crumble is crisp and golden.

To make the crème anglaise, place milk, cream, vanilla seeds and pod into a saucepan.

Heat over medium heat to almost boiling point before removing from the heat to cool slightly. Strain through a fine sieve and discard the vanilla pod.

Whisk the egg yolks and sugar together until thick and pale—the sugar must be dissolved.

Add ½ cup of the cream mixture to the egg mixture and beat continuously until combined, then add this to the remaining cream mixture, stirring continuously.

Return to a low–medium heat until it thickens.

Once thick, pass the crème anglaise through a sieve again into a large bowl.

Add ground cardamom to taste. Stir until combined and then transfer to a jug for serving.

To assemble, square a piece of the crumble and place on the centre of the plate, add three segments of blood orange and serve the crème anglaise in a pouring jug to the side.

SAGO WITH BLACK SESAME CRISP

SERVES 4

SAGO

2 purple dragon fruit
*200 ml/7 fl oz coconut
milk*
250 ml/9 fl oz water
180 g/6 oz sago
*120 g/4 oz caster/
superfine sugar*

SESAME CRISP

*100 g/3½ oz butter, at
room temperature*
*110 g/3½ oz caster/
superfine sugar*
*7 tablespoons packed
light brown sugar*
*60 g/2 oz plain/all-
purpose flour*
juice from 1½ oranges
*3 tablespoons black
sesame seeds*

TO SERVE

*2 fresh mangoes,
cheeks cut off, peeled
and into slices*
*young coconut, flesh
scooped out into
pieces for serving on
top*
*100 ml/3½ fl oz
coconut milk, to serve*
4 lime cheeks, to serve

To make the sago, cut the dragon fruits into small pieces and set aside.

In a saucepan, bring water to the boil, add sago and cook for 5 minutes.

Remove from the heat and let the sago sit for a further 5 minutes. Drain and run under cold water to stop the cooking process.

At this stage, the sago should be translucent on the outside and white on the inside.

In another saucepan, bring the 250 ml/9 fl oz of water to a boil, add the sugar and stir until dissolved.

Add the cooked sago and simmer on a low heat and then stir in the coconut milk and dragon fruits. Turn off the heat after 5–6 minutes.

To make the black sesame crisp, cream the butter until light and creamy. Add the sugar and continue to beat on medium speed for about 1 minute.

Turn the speed to low and add the flour. Mix well until combined. Slowly drizzle in the orange juice and mix for about 30 seconds.

Transfer the batter to an airtight container and refrigerate for as long as possible (1 hour is enough).

Preheat the oven to 175°C/350°F and position the rack to the centre of the oven.

Line a flat baking tray with baking paper (this batter spreads a lot, so make sure you have a very flat baking tray)

Pinch off a rounded tablespoon-size ball of dough and place on the tray. Repeat with the remaining mixture, spacing the balls at least 3 in apart from each other, allowing room to spread. Sprinkle with sesame seeds

Bake for 16–18 minutes or until crisps are golden brown. Let cool completely on the baking tray and then gently remove.

Serve sago in a clear glass bowl, place slices of mango and young coconut flesh in the centre of the sago. Drizzle over some coconut milk. Top with a black sesame crisp and a lime cheek to serve.

PEACH AND THYME ICE POPS

MAKES 6-12

8 fresh peaches, thinly
   sliced
2 cups water
²/₃ cup raw sugar
2 tablespoons honey
2 teaspoons fresh
   lemon juice
½ teaspoon lemon zest
1 teaspoon fresh thyme
1 cup champagne

In a saucepan, combine the peach slices, water and the sugar, mixing well until the sugar is dissolved.

Bring to a boil and simmer for 15 minutes.

Remove from the heat and stir in honey, lemon juice, zest and fresh thyme.

Set the mixture aside to cool for about 10 minutes.

Pour the mixture into a food processor and puree until smooth. Add champagne, cover and allow to chill in the fridge for 3 hours.

Pour the liquid into ice pop moulds and refrigerate until frozen.

STICKY DATE 'SCRONES'

FILLING
2 cups chopped dates
½ cup water
½ cup brown sugar
1–2 teaspoons mixed
  spice

SCONE BATTER
3 cups self-raising/self-
  rising flour, sifted
½ teaspoon baking
  powder
75 g/2½ oz cold butter,
  cubed
½ cup caster/superfine
  sugar
1 cup milk

SALTED CARAMEL
SAUCE
1 cup brown sugar
¼ cup water
¾ cup cream
3½ tablespoons
  unsalted butter
salt, to taste

These 'scrones' are half-way between a scone and a scroll. Filled with delicious dates and smothered in a salted caramel sauce, these are truly decadent.

To make the filling, combine all the ingredients in a saucepan over a medium-high heat. Bring to a boil, allow the sugar to dissolve and cook until the dates are soft. Allow the mixture to cool before using.

Preheat the oven to 180°C/350°F.

In a food processor, add the flour, baking powder and butter and pulse until it resembles breadcrumbs. Add the sugar and pulse a little. Add the milk and pulse until it all comes together.

Turn the dough out onto a lightly floured surface. Gently knead the dough to bring it together, then roll out about 1 cm/½ in thick.

Pour the filling onto the dough and spread out, leaving about 1.5 cm/½ in around the edges. Roll the dough up like a scroll. Then with a sharp knife, slice the scroll log into about 3 cm/1½ in slices. It should now look like scrolls. Place each slice onto a baking tray lined with baking paper, keeping them close together. This ensures they don't unroll while baking and helps them rise. Bake for 15–20 minutes, until golden brown.

To make the sauce, combine the sugar and water in a saucepan over a medium–low heat until the sugar is dissolved. Increase the heat and allow the mixture to boil, but do not stir.

Allow to boil until the sauce turns an amber colour. Take off the heat and whisk in the cream. Then add butter and salt to taste.

Serve the scrones while they are still warm from the oven, drizzled with a generous amount of salted caramel sauce.

HONEY SWEET DUMPLINGS
WITH RHUBARB

SWEET DUMPLINGS

3 cups plain/all-purpose flour

2/3 cups natural yoghurt

pinch of salt

½ teaspoon caster/superfine sugar

2 teaspoons yeast

1 litre/2 pints vegetable oil, for frying

honey, warmed and runny

RHUBARB COMPOTE

125 ml/4 fl oz water

3½ oz/100 g caster/superfine sugar

1 vanilla bean

1 cinnamon stick

8 cm strip of lemon zest

1 bunch of trimmed rhubarb cut into 1 in/2 cm pieces

250 g/9 oz strawberries, halved

To make the dumplings, mix the flour with the yoghurt. Add a pinch of salt and enough water to make a thick batter.

Combine the yeast and the sugar. Mix in ½ cup of warm water and allow the sugar to dissolve and the yeast to activate.

Pour the yeast mixture into the batter and stir to combine. Cover with a tea towel and set aside until the batter rises.

Heat the oil in a deep saucepan for frying.

Divide the batter into small balls.

Deep-fry the balls, a couple at a time, until golden brown. Remove and place onto paper towel.

Heat up some honey in a saucepan until runny, place cooked balls into honey and roll around to coat.

To make the rhubarb compote, place water and sugar in a saucepan over a low heat and allow to dissolve.

Add a vanilla bean, cinnamon stick and the lemon zest. Increase the heat to medium and bring to a boil for 4 minutes. Reduce the heat to low.

Add the trimmed rhubarb and strawberries. Allow to simmer until their shape starts to soften.

Remove from heat and allow to cool.

Remove the cinnamon stick, vanilla bean and lemon zest prior to serving.

To serve, place a few tablespoons of vanilla yoghurt onto a plate and spread around. Place five honey-coated dumplings on yoghurt randomly, spoon small amounts of compote onto the yoghurt and around the plate, making sure to have some chunky pieces and swirl compote into the yoghurt.

Dumplings are best when served warm. Sprinkle the top of each dumpling with some finely chopped pistachios and some colourful edible flower petals (orange, yellow and purple).

Serve with vanilla yoghurt, finely chopped pistachios and colourful edible flower petals of orange, purple, pink and yellow.

Notes

Dumplings are to be made and fried fresh. Dumplings are best served immediately and warm.

If you can, make the compote the day prior—it allows the spices to infuse.

CARROT AND COCONUT
GLUTEN-FREE LOAF

MAKES 1 LOAF

4 eggs

1 teaspoon vanilla paste

160 g/5½ oz coconut
  oil

4 mashed bananas

1½ cups almond meal

2 teaspoons baking
  soda

1 teaspoon ground
  cinnamon

1 cup chopped dates

1 cup grated carrot

½ cup desiccated
  coconut

½ cup dried cranberries

½ pistachios, shelled

Preheat the oven to 180°C/350°F. Grease and line a loaf tin with baking paper.

Whisk the eggs in a large bowl. Add vanilla, coconut oil and mashed bananas.

In a separate bowl, combine the almond meal, baking soda and ground cinnamon.

Add the wet ingredients to the dry ingredients and then fold in the dates, carrot, coconut, cranberries and nuts.

Transfer the mixture to the loaf tin and bake for 35–40 minutes, until a skewer comes out clean.

LEMON THYME SHORTBREAD

120 g/4 oz unsalted butter

55 g/2 oz caster/superfine sugar

zest of 2 lemons

3 tablespoons lemon thyme, leaves only

100 g/3½ oz plain/all-purpose flour

70 g/2½ oz rice flour

extra caster/superfine sugar, for dusting

Preheat the oven to 150°C/300°F. Grease and line a baking tray with baking paper. You could also grease a fluted tray, to give the edges of shortbread a pretty detail.

Beat the butter, sugar, lemon zest and thyme leaves together until pale and creamy.

Beat in the flour until a stiff dough forms.

Scrape the dough out of the bowl and into the baking tray. Press the dough into the tray firmly and work out to the edges. Smooth the top. Work quickly as the butter will begin to melt.

Bake in the oven for 15–20 minutes or until the edges are just golden. The shortbread will be a pale colour, not golden brown and a little soft to the touch.

GRANOLA BAR

4 cups oats

1 cup superfine/caster
  sugar

1 teaspoon salt

1 teaspoon ground
  cinnamon

6 cups dried fruit
  (cranberries, dates,
  sultanas)

2/3 cup peanut butter

1 cup coconut

2 teaspoons vanilla
  paste

240 g/8½ oz melted
  butter

1 cup honey

2 tablespoons water

Preheat the oven to 180°C/350°F. Grease and line a rectangular baking tray.

Combine all the dry ingredients in a bowl.

In a separate bowl, combine the water, vanilla, melted butter and honey.

Add the wet ingredients to the dry and stir in the peanut butter. Mix well.

Pour into the lined tray and press firmly.

Bake the bars for 30–35 minutes until the edges are lightly browned. Remove from the oven and leave to cool in the tray. Once cool, cut into the length you'd prefer.

INDEX